I0096806

The
CONSTITUTION
for
POLITICIANS

M. L. Rusciak

The Constitution for Politicians

The Constitution for Politicians

Trient Press
3375 S Rainbow Blvd
#81710, SMB 13135
Las Vegas,NV 89180

Ordering Information:
Quantity sales. Special discounts are available on quantity purchases by corporations, associations, and others. For details, contact the publisher at the address above.
Orders by U.S. trade bookstores and wholesalers. Please contact Trient Press: Tel: (775) 996-3844; or visit www.trientpress.com.

Printed in the United States of America

Publisher's Cataloging-in-Publication data
Ruscsak, M.L.
A title of a book :The Constitution for Politicians
ISBN
Paperback   978-1-955198-04-2

E-book   978-1-955198-03-5

The Constitution for Politicians

CHAPTER 1: PREAMBLE

❖   The importance of setting out the purpose and goals of the Constitution

❖   The humorous side of "We the People"

❖   An exploration of the historical context surrounding the creation of the Constitution and the motivations of the founding fathers

❖   A discussion of the principles of government and democracy that the Constitution embodies

❖   A breakdown of the Preamble sentence by sentence, highlighting the key goals and purposes laid out in each phrase

❖   A comparison of the language and tone used in the Preamble to that of other famous documents or speeches, such as the Declaration of Independence or the Gettysburg Address

❖   An examination of the various ways in which the Preamble has been used or referenced in pop culture, from movies and TV shows to music and literature

❖   Interviews or quotes from contemporary politicians or public figures discussing their own interpretations or reactions to the Preamble

❖   A summary of the ways in which the goals and purposes laid out in the Preamble have been fulfilled or challenged throughout American history, with examples ranging from the Civil War to modern-day debates about healthcare or climate change.

Greetings, dear reader! Are you ready to embark on a journey through the Preamble of the US Constitution? Buckle up, because we're about to dive into some serious history and politics... or not!

You see, the Preamble is not just a boring legal text full of legalese and Latin phrases. It's also a surprisingly fun and quirky document, full of interesting tidbits and hidden gems. Who knew that a simple phrase like "We the People" could be so delightfully ambiguous and multifaceted?

The Constitution for Politicians

So, put on your thinking cap, and get ready to explore the historical context, the motivations of the founding fathers, and the humorous side of the Preamble. We'll also delve into pop culture references, from movies to music, and examine the ways in which the Preamble has been used and misused throughout American history.

By the end of this chapter, you'll have a newfound appreciation for this tiny but mighty piece of text, and a deeper understanding of the goals and purposes laid out in the Preamble. So, let's get started!

The importance of setting out the purpose and goals of the Constitution

The United States Constitution is one of the most important documents in American history. It sets out the framework for the federal government and establishes the basic rights and freedoms that all Americans are entitled to. One of the most significant aspects of the Constitution is the way in which it lays out the purpose and goals of the new government that it creates. In this chapter, we will explore why this aspect of the Constitution is so important, both from a historical perspective and in terms of its ongoing relevance in American politics today.

The Importance of the Preamble

The Preamble to the Constitution is perhaps the most famous passage in the entire document. It reads as follows:

"We the People of the United States, in Order to form a more perfect Union, establish Justice, insure domestic Tranquility, provide for the common defence, promote the general Welfare, and secure the Blessings of Liberty to ourselves and our Posterity, do ordain and establish this Constitution for the United States of America."

This passage is so well-known that it has become something of a cultural touchstone, appearing in movies, television shows, and political speeches. But why is the Preamble so important, and what does it tell us about the purpose and goals of the Constitution?

The Constitution for Politicians

First and foremost, the Preamble sets out the overarching purpose of the Constitution. It makes clear that the goal of the document is to create a stronger and more unified country, one that is capable of protecting the rights and freedoms of its citizens. By laying out this goal at the very beginning of the Constitution, the framers were able to establish a clear sense of direction for the new government that they were creating.

But the Preamble goes beyond just setting out a broad purpose for the Constitution. It also lays out specific goals that the new government is expected to achieve. These goals are enumerated in the rest of the Preamble's famous sentence, which mentions "establishing Justice," "insuring domestic Tranquility," "providing for the common defence," "promoting the general Welfare," and "securing the Blessings of Liberty to ourselves and our Posterity." Each of these goals is significant in its own right, and they collectively represent a comprehensive vision for the role that the federal government should play in American society.

The Importance of Setting Out Goals in a Constitution

The idea of setting out goals and purposes in a constitution was not a new one when the United States Constitution was written. In fact, many of the state constitutions that preceded the federal Constitution had already taken this approach. But the framers of the federal Constitution recognized that, given the size and complexity of the new government they were creating, it was especially important to set out clear goals and purposes in the Constitution itself.

One reason for this is that the federal government created by the Constitution was, by design, much stronger and more centralized than the state governments that had preceded it. As a result, there was a greater need for the federal government to have a clear sense of direction and purpose. Without this, the new government would have been at risk of becoming unwieldy and ineffective.

But setting out goals and purposes in a constitution has benefits beyond just ensuring the effectiveness of the government. It also helps to establish a sense of unity and shared purpose among the people who are governed by the constitution. When a constitution sets out clear goals and purposes, it gives the people a sense of what they are working towards and what they can expect from their government. This, in turn, can help to build trust and cooperation between the government and its citizens.

The importance of setting out clear goals and purposes in a constitution is just as relevant in American politics today as it was when the Constitution was written. In fact, many of the debates that are happening in American politics today revolve around questions of what the goals and purposes of the government should be.

One area where this is particularly true is in the debate over the role of government in promoting economic growth and addressing income inequality. Some argue that the government should take an active role in addressing these issues, through programs like progressive taxation, social welfare programs, and investments in infrastructure and education. Others argue that the government should have a more limited role in these areas, leaving the market to allocate resources and create growth.

Another area where goals and purposes are central to the debate is in the realm of foreign policy. Some argue that the primary goal of American foreign policy should be to promote democracy and human rights around the world, while others argue that the primary goal should be to advance American economic and security interests.

These debates over the goals and purposes of government are likely to continue for as long as democracy itself exists. But the importance of setting out clear goals and purposes in a constitution remains constant. Without this, it is impossible to build a government that is effective, accountable, and responsive to the needs of its citizens.

Conclusion

The United States Constitution is a remarkable document, one that has stood the test of time and served as a model for democracies around the world. One of the reasons for its success is the way in which it sets out clear goals and purposes for the federal government that it creates. By doing so, the Constitution provides a roadmap for the new government, establishes a sense of direction and purpose for the American people, and helps to ensure that the government is effective, accountable, and responsive to the needs of its citizens. In short, the Constitution demonstrates the importance of setting out clear goals and purposes in any system of government, both for the sake of effectiveness and for the sake of democratic legitimacy.

The humorous side of "We the People"

We the People. It's a phrase that rolls off the tongue like a majestic waterfall, isn't it? But beyond its grandeur, there's also a comical side to this phrase that we can't help but poke fun at.

For one, "We the People" has become a popular slogan for t-shirts, bumper stickers, and all sorts of knick-knacks. People have taken it to absurd lengths, with slogans like "We the People...like to party" or "We the People...want tacos." These uses play on the idea of the people as a collective entity with a shared sense of identity and purpose, but also highlight the humor in reducing that identity and purpose to something as simple as a craving for tacos.

But the humor doesn't end there. "We the People" has been interpreted and reinterpreted so many times that it's taken on a life of its own. Some have taken to interpreting it in the most ridiculous ways possible. Satirical news site The Onion once ran a headline that read "We the People of the United States, in Order to Form a More Perfect Onion, Establish Onion Justice, Ensure Onion Domestic Tranquility..." It's a silly take on the way that "We the People" can be used to justify almost anything.

The phrase has also been used to create a sense of unity and solidarity among Americans. In times of crisis, it can be used to rally people together and create a sense of shared purpose. But this also opens the phrase up to humorous or satirical uses, as comedians and satirists use it to poke fun at the way that Americans come together in times of crisis.

But let's not forget the importance of "We the People." It's a phrase that embodies the idea of democracy and the power of the people to govern themselves. It's a reminder that the government exists to serve the people, not the other way around. And it's a call to action for all Americans to participate in their democracy and help shape the course of their country.

In the end, "We the People" may be a serious and important phrase, but that doesn't mean we can't have a little fun with it. So the next time you see someone wearing a "We the People...want tacos" t-shirt, take a moment to chuckle. But also remember the power and importance of this phrase. Because when it comes down to it, "We the People" is a call to action for all of us to come together and shape the future of our great nation.

Despite the humorous side of "We the People," it remains an important and powerful phrase in American political culture. It embodies the idea of democracy and the power of the people to govern themselves. It is a reminder that the government exists to serve the people, not the other way around. And it is a call to action for all Americans to participate in their democracy and help shape the course of their country.

Conclusion

"We the People" may be a serious and important phrase, but there is also a humorous side to it. From its use in popular culture to the absurd interpretations that it has inspired, "We the People" is a phrase that can be both powerful and funny. But at its core, it remains a reminder of the importance of democracy and the power of the people to govern themselves. It is a call to action for all Americans to take an active role in their democracy and help shape the course of their country.

An exploration of the historical context surrounding the creation of the

Constitution and the motivations of the founding fathers

So, you've read the Constitution, but do you really know why it was created? What were the motivations of the founding fathers? What historical events and contexts led up to the creation of this seminal document? Let's explore these questions together.

To start, let's rewind to the late 18th century. The thirteen colonies had just won their independence from Great Britain after years of fighting and sacrifice. But the aftermath of the revolution was messy. The Articles of Confederation, which were the governing document at the time, were weak and ineffective. The country was struggling with debt, economic depression, and political disunity. It was clear that something needed to change.

And so, in 1787, a group of delegates gathered in Philadelphia to draft a new governing document. This document, of course, would become the Constitution. But what motivated these delegates to create this new document? Why did they feel that the Articles of Confederation were insufficient?

There were a few key motivations at play. For one, the delegates were deeply concerned with preserving the unity of the newly-formed nation. They recognized that the Articles of Confederation did not provide a strong enough framework for this unity, and that a more centralized and powerful government was necessary to ensure the country's stability.

But there were also other motivations at play. The founding fathers were influenced by the Enlightenment ideals of liberty, democracy, and individual rights. They saw the Constitution as a way to protect and enshrine these ideals in law. They were also influenced by the political philosophies of figures like John Locke and Montesquieu, who advocated for the separation of powers and checks and balances within government.

Of course, it's also important to consider the historical context in which the Constitution was created. The delegates were grappling with the legacy of British colonial rule, as well as the challenges of forging a new national identity. They were also grappling with issues of slavery and representation, which would shape the debates around the Constitution and its eventual compromises.

In the end, the Constitution represented a delicate balance of competing interests and motivations. It was a document designed to preserve the unity and stability of a young nation, while also upholding the ideals of democracy, liberty, and individual rights. It was a document influenced by the political philosophies of the Enlightenment, as well as the specific historical context of the time.

But the story of the Constitution doesn't end there. It has been revised, amended, and debated countless times over the centuries. It has been challenged, questioned, and reinterpreted by successive generations of Americans. And yet, it endures as a testament to the founding fathers' vision for a united, democratic, and free nation.

So, the next time you read the Constitution, take a moment to think about the historical context and motivations that led to its creation. Remember that it was a document crafted by humans with complex motivations and ideals, but one that has endured and shaped the course of American history.

A breakdown of the Preamble sentence by sentence, highlighting the key goals and purposes laid out in each phrase

The Preamble of the Constitution is the introductory statement to the United States Constitution. It begins with the famous words, "We the People of the United States," and goes on to set out the fundamental purposes and goals of the Constitution.

The full text of the Preamble is as follows:

"We the People of the United States, in Order to form a more perfect Union, establish Justice, insure domestic Tranquility, provide for the common defense, promote the general Welfare, and secure the

The Constitution for Politicians

Blessings of Liberty to ourselves and our Posterity, do ordain and establish this Constitution for the United States of America."

In essence, the Preamble serves as a mission statement for the Constitution. It lays out the reasons why the Constitution was written, and what the Founding Fathers hoped to achieve through its creation. Some of the key goals and purposes outlined in the Preamble include:

✧   Forming a more perfect union: This refers to the desire of the Founding Fathers to create a stronger, more unified country than the loose confederation that had existed under the Articles of Confederation.

✧   Establishing justice: This refers to the desire to create a fair and equitable system of laws and courts that would protect the rights of all citizens.

✧   Insuring domestic tranquility: This refers to the desire to maintain peace and order within the country, and to prevent domestic unrest or rebellion.

✧   Providing for the common defense: This refers to the desire to create a strong military and defense system that would protect the country from foreign threats.

✧   Promoting the general welfare: This refers to the desire to create policies and programs that would benefit all citizens, such as public education, infrastructure projects, and social safety nets.

✧   Securing the blessings of liberty: This refers to the desire to protect the individual freedoms and rights of all citizens, both now and in the future.

Overall, the Preamble sets out a lofty and ambitious set of goals for the Constitution. It reflects the deep commitment of the Founding Fathers to creating a fair, just, and prosperous society, and serves as a reminder of the enduring values and principles that underlie American democracy.

Let's take a closer look at the Preamble of the Constitution, shall we? This sentence is just one long sentence, but it packs a lot of meaning into those few words. So, let's break it down phrase by phrase, and explore the key goals and purposes laid out in each.

First up: "We the people of the United States." This phrase sets the tone for the entire document. It emphasizes that the Constitution is a product of the people, not just a group of elites or politicians. It's a reminder that this document is meant to serve the needs and interests of all Americans, not just a select few.

Next, we have "in order to form a more perfect union." This phrase emphasizes the need for unity and cooperation among the states. Remember, at the time of the Constitution's creation, the country was still a young and fragile union. The founding fathers recognized that a strong, centralized government was necessary to ensure the stability and success of the nation.

Moving on: "establish justice." This phrase speaks to the importance of a fair and just legal system. It emphasizes the idea that all individuals, regardless of their background or status, should be held accountable under the law. It's a powerful reminder that the Constitution is meant to protect the rights and freedoms of all Americans, not just a select few.

Next up: "insure domestic tranquility." This phrase emphasizes the need for peace and stability within the country. The founding fathers recognized that a stable and secure society was necessary for the success of the nation. This phrase speaks to the importance of social harmony, and the need to maintain a sense of order and safety within the country.

Moving along: "provide for the common defense." This phrase speaks to the importance of national security. It's a reminder that the government has a responsibility to protect its citizens, both at home and abroad. The phrase also emphasizes the idea that the government should be prepared to act in the face of threats to national security.

Finally, we have "promote the general welfare and secure the blessings of liberty to ourselves and our posterity." This phrase is perhaps the most expansive and far-reaching of the entire Preamble. It speaks to the importance of promoting the well-being and prosperity of all Americans, both now and in the future. It emphasizes the importance of individual liberty and freedom, while also acknowledging the responsibility that we have to future generations.

Taken together, these phrases paint a powerful picture of the goals and purposes of the Constitution. They emphasize the importance of unity, justice, peace, security, and prosperity. They remind us that the Constitution is meant to serve the needs and interests of all Americans, not just a select few. And they underscore the importance of individual liberty and freedom, as well as our collective responsibility to protect and promote the well-being of future generations.

So, the next time you read the Preamble, take a moment to reflect on the profound goals and purposes that are laid out in those few words. Remember that this document has served as a cornerstone of American democracy and freedom for over two centuries, and that its principles continue to guide us today.

A comparison of the language and tone used in the Preamble to that of other famous documents or speeches, such as the Declaration of Independence or the Gettysburg Address

First, let's look at the language and tone used in the Preamble. As we've already discussed, the Preamble is a powerful and concise statement of the goals and purposes of the Constitution. It's written in a clear and direct style, with an emphasis on unity, justice, peace, security, and prosperity for all Americans. The tone is one of optimism and hope, but also of seriousness and purpose.

Now, let's compare this to the language and tone used in the Declaration of Independence. This document, written over a decade before the Constitution, is perhaps the most famous statement of

The Constitution for Politicians

American ideals and principles. The Declaration of Independence is written in a much more poetic and flowery style than the Preamble. It's full of powerful, evocative phrases like "life, liberty, and the pursuit of happiness," and "We hold these truths to be self-evident." The tone is one of outrage and defiance, as the colonists declare their independence from Great Britain and assert their natural rights as human beings.

Moving on to the Gettysburg Address, we find another famous American speech that speaks to the values and principles of the country. The Gettysburg Address is much shorter than either the Preamble or the Declaration of Independence, but it packs a powerful emotional punch. It's written in a simple, direct style, with an emphasis on unity, sacrifice, and the importance of the individual. The tone is one of solemnity and reverence, as President Lincoln pays tribute to the soldiers who gave their lives in defense of the Union.

So, what can we learn from these comparisons? Well, first of all, we can see that the language and tone of American political documents and speeches has evolved over time. The Preamble, written over a decade after the Declaration of Independence, is much more direct and pragmatic in its style and tone. The Gettysburg Address, written over half a century after the Constitution, is even more concise and emotionally powerful than either of the earlier documents.

But despite these differences, there are also some common themes and values that run through all of these documents. Unity, justice, peace, security, and individual liberty are all emphasized in different ways, but they remain central to the American political tradition. And although the language and tone of these documents may change over time, the underlying values and principles remain constant.

So, whether you're reading the Preamble, the Declaration of Independence, or the Gettysburg Address, take a moment to appreciate the unique language and tone of each document. But also remember that these documents all speak to the same fundamental values and principles that have guided American democracy for over two centuries.

An examination of the various ways in which the Preamble has been used or referenced in pop culture, from movies and TV shows to music and literature

The Preamble of the Constitution may be a serious and weighty document, but that hasn't stopped it from making appearances in popular culture over the years. From movies and TV shows to music and literature, the Preamble has been referenced and used in a variety of ways, often with a humorous or satirical twist.

One example of the Preamble being used in pop culture is in the opening credits of the classic television show "Schoolhouse Rock!" In the segment "Preamble," a group of singers performs a catchy tune that breaks down the key phrases of the Preamble into easy-to-understand lyrics. This musical rendition of the Preamble has become a beloved cultural touchstone, and is often cited by educators as a fun and engaging way to teach students about the Constitution.

Another example of the Preamble appearing in pop culture is in the 1995 movie "The American President." In the film, the character played by Michael Douglas delivers a rousing speech in which he quotes the Preamble and argues that America must live up to its founding principles of liberty and justice for all. This scene has become a classic moment in American cinema, and is often cited as an example of how the Preamble can inspire and motivate people to action.

The Preamble has also been referenced in various forms of literature, from children's books to political satire. For example, the book "We the Kids" by David Catrow uses humorous illustrations to explain the meaning of the Preamble to young readers. Similarly, the comic strip "Doonesbury" has featured numerous references to the Preamble over the years, often using it as a way to comment on current events or political issues.

In addition to these examples, the Preamble has also been referenced in a variety of music genres, from rock and roll to hip hop. The band Rage Against the Machine, for instance, has used the text of the Preamble as a lyrical hook in their song "Freedom." Similarly, rapper Nas has referenced the Preamble in his song "America," using it as a jumping-off point for a critique of contemporary American society.

Despite the many humorous and irreverent uses of the Preamble in pop culture, it's important to remember the serious and weighty significance of this document. As a foundational text of American democracy, the Preamble lays out the core principles and values that underlie our system of government. By understanding and appreciating the Preamble, we can gain a deeper appreciation for the ideals that have shaped our country for over two centuries.

The Legacy of the Preamble: Achievements and Challenges in American History

The Preamble of the Constitution lays out the goals and purposes of the document, and by extension, the principles and values that underlie the American system of government. Throughout American history, these goals and purposes have been both fulfilled and challenged, with important consequences for the nation and its people.

One of the most dramatic examples of the fulfillment and challenge of the goals and purposes of the Preamble came during the Civil War. The conflict was fought over the very question of whether America could truly be a nation dedicated to the principles of liberty, justice, and equality for all. The Union ultimately prevailed, but the scars of the war and the continued struggle for civil rights have shown that the Preamble's goals and purposes are not always easy to achieve.

Another area where the Preamble's goals and purposes have been challenged is in the realm of healthcare. While the document speaks of promoting the general welfare of the American people, the issue of healthcare has been a contentious one for decades. Debates over the proper role of government in providing healthcare have been heated, with proponents arguing that it is a fundamental right, and opponents arguing that it is not the government's responsibility.

Similarly, the issue of climate change has become a key challenge to the goals and purposes of the Preamble in recent years. While the document speaks of securing the blessings of liberty for ourselves and our posterity, the effects of climate change threaten to undermine those blessings in a number of ways. Rising sea levels, extreme weather events, and other consequences of climate change pose a threat to the health, safety, and well-being of Americans, as well as to the future of the planet.

Throughout American history, however, there have also been many examples of the Preamble's goals and purposes being fulfilled. The establishment of a system of public education, for instance, can be seen as a fulfillment of the document's aim to promote the general welfare of the American people. Similarly, the Civil Rights Movement of the mid-20th century, which fought for equal rights and justice for all Americans, can be seen as a fulfillment of the document's aim to secure the blessings of liberty for ourselves and our posterity.

Another area where the Preamble's goals and purposes have been fulfilled is in the realm of international relations. America has long been a leader in promoting democracy, human rights, and the rule of law around the world, and has played a key role in helping to create a more peaceful and prosperous global community.

The Preamble of the Constitution remains an important document in American history, and its goals and purposes continue to shape the nation and its people. While there have been many challenges to the fulfillment of these goals and purposes, there have also been many examples of their achievement. By understanding the legacy of the Preamble, we can gain a deeper appreciation for the principles and values that have guided America for over two centuries, and continue to do so today.

The Constitution for Politicians

In conclusion, the Preamble to the US Constitution is not just a string of words. It is a powerful declaration of the values, goals, and aspirations that guided the founding fathers in their quest to create a more perfect union. By breaking down each sentence of the Preamble, we have gained a better understanding of the importance of setting out the purpose and goals of the Constitution, and the ways in which it has shaped the course of American history. We have also explored the humorous side of "We the People," as well as the various ways in which the Preamble has been used or referenced in pop culture. Finally, we have examined the challenges and triumphs in fulfilling the goals and purposes of the Preamble throughout American history.

As we move forward, it is important to remember that the Preamble is not just a relic of the past. It is a living document that continues to inspire us and guide us in our pursuit of a more perfect union. It is a reminder of the values and principles that make America great, and a call to action for all Americans to work towards a brighter future for ourselves and future generations.

CHAPTER 2: ARTICLE I - THE LEGISLATIVE BRANCH

❖   The Break Down
❖   Overview of the House of Representatives and Senate
❖   The role of Congress in making laws
❖   Humorous anecdotes about past and present lawmakers
❖   Qualifications and terms of members of Congress
❖   Powers of Congress, including taxation, commerce, and defense

The Constitution for Politicians

- ❖ Procedures for passing laws
- ❖ Checks and balances on Congress
- ❖ Impeachment of federal officials

Article I of the United States Constitution outlines the structure and powers of the legislative branch of the federal government. Here is the full text of Article I:

Section 1:
All legislative Powers herein granted shall be vested in a Congress of the United States, which shall consist of a Senate and House of Representatives.

Section 2:
The House of Representatives shall be composed of Members chosen every second Year by the People of the several States, and the Electors in each State shall have the Qualifications requisite for Electors of the most numerous Branch of the State Legislature.

No Person shall be a Representative who shall not have attained to the Age of twenty-five Years, and been seven Years a Citizen of the United States, and who shall not, when elected, be an Inhabitant of that State in which he shall be chosen.

Representatives and direct Taxes shall be apportioned among the several States which may be included within this Union, according to their respective Numbers, which shall be determined by adding to the whole Number of free Persons, including those bound to Service for a Term of Years, and excluding Indians not taxed, three fifths of all other Persons.

The actual Enumeration shall be made within three Years after the first Meeting of the Congress of the United States, and within every subsequent Term of ten Years, in such Manner as they shall by Law direct. The Number of Representatives shall not exceed one for every thirty Thousand, but each State shall have at Least one Representative; and until such enumeration shall be made, the State of New Hampshire shall be entitled to choose three, Massachusetts eight, Rhode Island and Providence Plantations one, Connecticut five, New

The Constitution for Politicians

York six, New Jersey four, Pennsylvania eight, Delaware one, Maryland six, Virginia ten, North Carolina five, South Carolina five, and Georgia three.

When vacancies happen in the Representation from any State, the Executive Authority thereof shall issue Writs of Election to fill such Vacancies.

The House of Representatives shall choose their Speaker and other Officers; and shall have the sole Power of Impeachment.

Section 3:
The Senate of the United States shall be composed of two Senators from each State, chosen by the Legislature thereof, for six Years; and each Senator shall have one Vote.

Immediately after they shall be assembled in Consequence of the first Election, they shall be divided as equally as may be into three Classes. The Seats of the Senators of the first Class shall be vacated at the Expiration of the second Year, of the second Class at the Expiration of the fourth Year, and of the third Class at the Expiration of the sixth Year, so that one third may be chosen every second Year; and if Vacancies happen by Resignation, or otherwise, during the Recess of the Legislature of any State, the Executive thereof may make temporary Appointments until the next Meeting of the Legislature, which shall then fill such Vacancies.

No Person shall be a Senator who shall not have attained to the Age of thirty Years, and been nine Years a Citizen of the United States, and who shall not, when elected, be an Inhabitant of that State for which he shall be chosen.

The Vice President of the United States shall be President of the Senate, but shall have no Vote, unless they be equally divided.

The Senate shall choose their other Officers, and also a President pro tempore, in the absence of the Vice President, or when he shall exercise the Office of President of the United States.

The Senate shall have the sole Power to try all Impeachments. When sitting for that Purpose, they shall be on Oath or Affirmation. When the President of the United States is tried, the Chief Justice shall preside: And no Person shall be convicted without the Concurrence of two thirds of the Members

The break down

Section 1:
All legislative Powers herein granted shall be vested in a Congress of the United States, which shall consist of a Senate and House of Representatives.

According to Harvard Law School, Section 1 of Article I of the Constitution establishes the legislative branch of the federal government and vests all legislative powers in a bicameral Congress, consisting of a Senate and a House of Representatives. This provision sets out the basic structure and composition of the federal legislative body, and emphasizes the fundamental principle of separation of powers, which was intended to prevent any one branch of government from becoming too powerful or dominant. By vesting all legislative powers in Congress, the Constitution ensures that the people's elected representatives have the primary responsibility for making laws, and establishes a system of checks and balances to prevent any one branch of government from becoming too dominant or overreaching its authority. This provision has been interpreted by the courts to mean that Congress has broad authority to legislate on matters of national concern, subject to the limitations set forth in the Constitution and the Bill of Rights.

Section 2:
The House of Representatives shall be composed of Members chosen every second Year by the People of the several States, and the Electors in each State shall have the Qualifications requisite for Electors of the most numerous Branch of the State Legislature.

No Person shall be a Representative who shall not have attained to the Age of twenty-five Years, and been seven Years a Citizen of the United States, and who shall not, when elected, be an Inhabitant of that State in which he shall be chosen.

Representatives and direct Taxes shall be apportioned among the several States which may be included within this Union, according to their respective Numbers, which shall be determined by adding to the whole Number of free Persons, including those bound to Service for a Term of Years, and excluding Indians not taxed, three fifths of all other Persons.

The actual Enumeration shall be made within three Years after the first Meeting of the Congress of the United States, and within every subsequent Term of ten Years, in such Manner as they shall by Law direct. The Number of Representatives shall not exceed one for every thirty Thousand, but each State shall have at Least one Representative; and until such enumeration shall be made, the State of New Hampshire shall be entitled to choose three, Massachusetts eight, Rhode Island and Providence Plantations one, Connecticut five, New York six, New Jersey four, Pennsylvania eight, Delaware one, Maryland six, Virginia ten, North Carolina five, South Carolina five, and Georgia three.

When vacancies happen in the Representation from any State, the Executive Authority thereof shall issue Writs of Election to fill such Vacancies.

The House of Representatives shall choose their Speaker and other Officers; and shall have the sole Power of Impeachment.

Section 2 of Article I of the United States Constitution lays out the composition and responsibilities of the House of Representatives. The section begins by stating that members of the House will be elected every two years by the people of their respective states. The electors in each state must meet the qualifications required for electors of the most numerous branch of the state legislature.

Next, the section outlines the qualifications for being a representative. A person must have reached the age of 25, been a citizen of the United States for at least seven years, and be an inhabitant of the state they will represent at the time of their election.

The section goes on to explain how representation and taxes will be apportioned among the states. The number of representatives each state receives will be determined by adding the number of free persons and those bound to service for a term of years, while excluding Indians not taxed. Additionally, three-fifths of all other persons (i.e. slaves) will also be counted. This clause was later changed by the 14th Amendment, which abolished slavery and granted citizenship to all people born or naturalized in the United States, regardless of race.

An actual enumeration, or census, will be taken within three years of the first meeting of Congress and every ten years thereafter to determine the number of representatives for each state. The number of representatives shall not exceed one for every thirty thousand people, but each state must have at least one representative. Until the first census was taken, the number of representatives for each state was predetermined as follows: New Hampshire - 3, Massachusetts - 8, Rhode Island and Providence Plantations - 1, Connecticut - 5, New York - 6, New Jersey - 4, Pennsylvania - 8, Delaware - 1, Maryland - 6, Virginia - 10, North Carolina - 5, South Carolina - 5, and Georgia - 3.

The section also covers the procedure for filling vacancies in the House of Representatives. When a vacancy occurs in a state's representation, the executive authority of that state must issue writs of election to fill the vacancy.

Lastly, the section gives the House of Representatives the power to choose their Speaker and other officers, as well as the sole power of impeachment. This means that the House has the authority to bring charges of misconduct against federal officials, including the President and other members of the executive branch. If the House impeaches a federal official, the Senate then conducts a trial to determine whether to remove the official from office.

Section 3:

The Constitution for Politicians

Section 3 of the United States Constitution outlines the structure and powers of the Senate. The section is broken down into several paragraphs that each detail a specific aspect of the Senate.

The first paragraph states that the Senate is composed of two senators from each state, chosen by the legislature of that state, for a term of six years. Each senator is granted one vote, regardless of the population of the state they represent.

The second paragraph establishes a system of staggered elections. After the first election, senators will be divided into three classes as equally as possible. The terms of the senators in the first class will expire after two years, the terms of the senators in the second class will expire after four years, and the terms of the senators in the third class will expire after six years. This system ensures that the Senate is never completely replaced at one time and that there is always continuity in the legislative branch.

The third paragraph outlines the qualifications for senators. A person must be at least thirty years old, have been a citizen of the United States for at least nine years, and be a resident of the state they will represent at the time of their election.

The fourth paragraph establishes the role of the Vice President as the President of the Senate. However, the Vice President only has a vote in the Senate if the votes are tied. The President pro tempore is chosen by the Senate and serves as the presiding officer in the absence of the Vice President or if the Vice President is serving as the President of the United States.

The fifth and final paragraph gives the Senate the sole power to try all impeachments. During impeachment trials, senators are required to take an oath or affirmation. If the President of the United States is being tried, the Chief Justice of the Supreme Court will preside. Conviction requires the concurrence of two-thirds of the members present.

The Constitution for Politicians

Overall, Section 3 establishes the structure, powers, and responsibilities of the Senate, which serves as a crucial part of the legislative branch of the United States government.

For Students:

So the Constitution of the United States is like the rule book for our country. It has three parts that talk about how the Congress works. Congress is the group of people who make the laws for our country.

The first part is called Section 1. It says that all the people who make the laws, called the legislative powers, are in a group called Congress. There are two parts of Congress, the Senate and the House of Representatives.

The second part is called Section 2. It talks about the House of Representatives. The House of Representatives is made up of people who are elected every two years by the people who live in each state. They have to be at least 25 years old, a citizen of the United States for at least 7 years, and live in the state where they were chosen.

The number of people in the House of Representatives depends on how many people live in each state. Every state gets at least one person, but bigger states get more. The number of people is counted every 10 years, and it's called a census.

If someone in the House of Representatives leaves their job, then the state governor has to choose someone else to take their place until the next election. The House of Representatives also gets to choose who can be impeached, which means kicked out of office.

The third part is called Section 3. It talks about the Senate. The Senate is made up of two people from each state. They are chosen by the state legislature, which is a group of people who work for the state government. Senators have to be at least 30 years old, a citizen of the United States for at least 9 years, and live in the state they were chosen for.

Senators are in the job for 6 years, but every two years one-third of the Senators have to be elected again. The Vice President of the United States is also the leader of the Senate, but he can only vote if there's a tie.

The Senate gets to choose who can be impeached too. But when they're doing an impeachment trial, they have to swear an oath that they'll be fair. If the President of the United States is being impeached, then the Chief Justice of the Supreme Court gets to be the judge instead of the Vice President.

So that's the basics of how Congress works!

Overview of the House of Representatives and Senate

Welcome to Chapter 2, where we'll take a closer look at the two branches of the United States Congress: the House of Representatives and the Senate.

First things first: what's the difference between the House and the Senate? Well, they both make up Congress, but they have different roles and functions. The House of Representatives is the lower chamber of Congress, with 435 voting members representing districts in each state. The number of representatives for each state is determined by population, with each state having at least one representative.

The Senate, on the other hand, is the upper chamber of Congress, with 100 members representing each state equally, regardless of population. Each state has two senators, and they serve six-year terms.

Now, let's take a closer look at the House of Representatives. The main function of the House is to represent the people, and they are often referred to as the "people's house." Members of the House are elected every two years, and they are responsible for introducing and passing bills that address issues such as taxes, healthcare, and education. The Speaker of the House is the leader of the House, and is responsible for guiding the legislative agenda and presiding over debates.

In addition to their legislative duties, members of the House also have certain powers and responsibilities, such as the power to impeach the President, and the power to introduce bills related to taxes and spending.

Now, let's turn our attention to the Senate. The Senate is often referred to as the "upper chamber," and has more deliberative powers than the House. One of the main responsibilities of the Senate is to approve presidential nominations for executive and judicial positions, including Supreme Court Justices.

The Senate also has the power to ratify treaties and conduct impeachment trials, with the Chief Justice of the Supreme Court presiding over the trial if the President is being impeached. The Senate also plays a role in passing legislation, but bills must first be passed by the House before they can be considered by the Senate.

So, to summarize: the House of Representatives is responsible for representing the people, passing bills related to issues such as taxes and healthcare, and has the power to impeach the President. The Senate, on the other hand, is responsible for approving presidential nominations, ratifying treaties, and conducting impeachment trials, and has a more deliberative role in passing legislation.

While the House and the Senate have different roles and functions, they work together to pass laws and represent the American people. In the next chapter, we'll take a closer look at the legislative process and how bills become laws.

The role of Congress in making laws

Congress, as the legislative branch of the United States government, is responsible for crafting and enacting laws that shape the country's policies, regulations, and governance. The process of creating legislation can be complex and lengthy, involving multiple steps and branches of government. Understanding the role of

The Constitution for Politicians

Congress in making laws is essential to comprehending the functioning of the American political system.

The Constitution grants Congress the power to make laws in Article I, Section 1, stating, "All legislative Powers herein granted shall be vested in a Congress of the United States, which shall consist of a Senate and House of Representatives." This simple sentence provides the foundation for the legislative process that shapes American politics.

The Constitution lays out the basic process for how a bill becomes a law, but the specifics of that process have evolved over time. The process typically begins when a member of Congress introduces a bill, which is then assigned to a committee for review. If the committee approves the bill, it moves on to the full House or Senate for debate and voting. If both the House and Senate approve the bill, it goes to the President for signature or veto.

One of the primary roles of Congress in making laws is to represent the interests and needs of the American people. Members of Congress are elected to their positions by the citizens of their districts or states, and they are accountable to those voters. As such, Congress has the responsibility to consider and address the concerns of the people they represent when crafting and enacting laws.

Congress also plays a critical role in creating laws that promote the public good and welfare. Many laws address issues that are of national importance, such as ensuring access to healthcare, protecting the environment, or promoting economic growth. Congress has the power to pass laws that help improve the lives of Americans and ensure that the country remains strong and prosperous.

In addition to crafting laws, Congress also has the authority to oversee and regulate the actions of the executive branch, which includes the President and federal agencies. Congress has the power to investigate and hold hearings on a wide range of issues, from foreign policy to domestic regulations. This oversight function helps ensure that the government operates in a transparent and accountable manner.

The Constitution for Politicians

One of the key aspects of the legislative process is compromise. Lawmaking is rarely a straightforward process, and often involves negotiations and compromises between different factions of Congress. Members of Congress may have differing views on a particular issue, but they must work together to craft a bill that can gain the support of enough members to pass.

The legislative process can be influenced by a wide range of factors, including public opinion, interest groups, and the media. Members of Congress must balance the needs and interests of their constituents with the broader goals and priorities of the country as a whole. This can sometimes result in tension and conflict, but it is an essential part of the democratic process.

Congress is also responsible for ensuring that the laws it creates are enforced. This includes providing funding for the agencies and programs that enforce the law, as well as monitoring their activities to ensure they are carrying out their duties in an effective and efficient manner.

Another critical function of Congress is to amend the Constitution when necessary. The Constitution is a living document that has been amended 27 times since its creation. Congress plays a critical role in this process, as amendments must be approved by both the House and Senate before they can be sent to the states for ratification.

In recent years, the legislative process has become more challenging, as polarization and partisanship have increased. Members of Congress are often pressured by their party leadership, interest groups, and constituents to vote in a particular way on issues, which can make it difficult to achieve compromise and consensus. However, the legislative process remains a critical part of American democracy, and the role of Congress in making laws continues to be essential.

One of the key aspects of the legislative process is the committee system. Committees are specialized groups within Congress that are responsible for studying and debating specific issues. There are standing committees, which are permanent and deal with particular subject areas, and ad hoc or select committees, which are created for a specific purpose and dissolved once their task is complete.

Committees provide an opportunity for members of Congress to focus on specific issues in more depth, hear from experts and stakeholders, and consider legislation in a more deliberative and informed manner. However, committees can also be used by party leadership to control the legislative process and advance their agenda.

Once a bill has been debated and passed out of committee, it is then considered by the full House or Senate. The rules governing debate and amendment vary between the two chambers. In the House, debate is usually limited, and amendments must be germane to the bill being considered. In the Senate, there is often more extensive debate, and senators have greater freedom to offer amendments.

The process of passing a bill can be long and complex. If the House and Senate pass different versions of a bill, a conference committee is appointed to work out the differences and produce a compromise bill that both chambers can agree on. Once a bill has been passed by both the House and Senate, it is sent to the President for approval. If the President signs the bill, it becomes law. If the President vetoes the bill, it can still become law if two-thirds of the House and Senate vote to override the veto.

In recent years, the legislative process has faced significant challenges. The increasing polarization and partisanship in Congress have made it difficult to achieve compromise and consensus. Gridlock and government shutdowns have become more common, and many important issues remain unresolved. Additionally, the influence of special interests and the role of money in politics have raised concerns about the ability of Congress to effectively represent the interests of the American people.

Despite these challenges, the legislative process remains a critical part of American democracy. The ability of Congress to make laws and represent the interests of the American people is essential to maintaining a functioning democratic system. The process of compromise and negotiation may be slow and frustrating, but it is necessary to ensure that the laws passed by Congress are in the best interest of the American people.

In conclusion, the role of Congress in making laws is essential to the functioning of American democracy. The legislative process, while often challenging and complex, provides an opportunity for elected representatives to debate and deliberate on important issues and work towards solutions that benefit the American people. While there are significant challenges facing Congress in the modern era, it is important to recognize the critical role that Congress plays in shaping the laws that govern our country.

Qualifications and terms of members of Congress

In order to be eligible to serve in the United States Congress, an individual must meet certain qualifications. These qualifications are laid out in the U.S. Constitution, which specifies that members of the House of Representatives and Senate must be at least 25 and 30 years old, respectively, and must have been a U.S. citizen for at least seven and nine years, respectively. Additionally, members of Congress must be residents of the state they represent.

The Constitution sets out these requirements to ensure that members of Congress are experienced, knowledgeable, and have a strong connection to their constituents. By requiring members to be citizens for at least seven or nine years, the framers of the Constitution also sought to prevent foreign influence in the legislative process.

Once elected, members of Congress serve terms that vary in length. Members of the House of Representatives serve two-year terms, while Senators serve six-year terms. This difference in term length was intended to ensure that the House, which is meant to be the more responsive and democratic of the two chambers, would be more sensitive to the views of the public, while the Senate, which was designed to be more deliberative and insulated from public opinion, would be able to take a longer-term view.

The terms of members of Congress are staggered so that only one-third of the Senate is up for election every two years. This means that the Senate is always composed of experienced members who have already served at least two years, and who can provide continuity and stability to the legislative process. At the same time, this system also ensures that the Senate is responsive to changes in the political landscape, as one-third of its members are elected every two years.

Another important feature of the U.S. Congress is that members can be reelected an unlimited number of times. This means that members can serve for decades, building up significant expertise and experience in the legislative process. However, it also means that some members may become entrenched in their positions, and may be more resistant to change or compromise.

The fact that members of Congress can serve for long periods of time also means that the composition of Congress can change gradually over time. This can have important implications for the legislative process, as changes in the makeup of Congress can alter the balance of power between the two parties, or between different factions within a party. For example, if one party gains a significant number of seats in Congress in a given election cycle, it may be able to push through legislation that was previously blocked by the opposing party.

In addition to these formal requirements and terms of service, there are also informal qualifications and expectations that shape who is elected to Congress and how they behave once they are in office. One important factor is political experience, including experience in state or local government, or in other branches of the federal government. This experience can be important in helping members navigate the complex legislative process, as well as in building relationships with other members of Congress and with key stakeholders outside of Congress.

Another important factor is fundraising ability. Because running for Congress is expensive, candidates who are able to raise large amounts of money are often more competitive in elections. This can create a situation in which members of Congress are more beholden to their donors than to their constituents, and can make it more difficult to pass legislation that is not favored by powerful interest groups.

Finally, there are also informal expectations regarding the behavior of members of Congress, including a commitment to public service, a willingness to work across the aisle to achieve common goals, and a dedication to upholding the principles and values of the U.S. Constitution. However, in recent years, these expectations have been challenged by a political climate that has become increasingly polarized and contentious.

Despite these challenges, members of Congress are still expected to conduct themselves in a manner befitting their position as elected representatives of the American people. This includes maintaining high ethical standards, avoiding conflicts of interest, and working diligently to serve the needs and interests of their constituents.

In terms of qualifications, the Constitution lays out several requirements for members of Congress. For the House of Representatives, members must be at least 25 years old, have been a citizen of the United States for at least seven years, and be a resident of the state they represent at the time of their election. For the Senate, members must be at least 30 years old, have been a citizen of the United States for at least nine years, and be a resident of the state they represent at the time of their election.

In addition to these constitutional requirements, there are also certain unwritten qualifications that are often considered when evaluating potential candidates for Congress. These may include prior experience in public service, a strong educational background, and a track record of community involvement and leadership.

Once elected, members of Congress serve terms of different lengths depending on their chamber. Representatives serve two-year terms, while senators serve six-year terms. This difference in term length is intended to provide the House of Representatives with more frequent turnover and greater responsiveness to changing public sentiment, while the longer terms of senators are meant to provide greater stability and continuity in policymaking.

Members of Congress are also subject to certain ethical and financial disclosure requirements, which are designed to ensure that they are acting in the best interests of the American people rather than their own personal interests. These include regular financial disclosure statements and restrictions on the acceptance of gifts or other forms of compensation that could be perceived as influencing their decision-making.

While the qualifications and terms of members of Congress may seem straightforward, they are often the subject of intense political debate and controversy. In recent years, there have been calls to impose additional requirements on members of Congress, such as term limits or mandatory retirement ages, in order to address concerns about career politicians and entrenched interests.

At the same time, there are also concerns that these types of reforms could limit the ability of experienced legislators to make meaningful contributions to the policymaking process, and could potentially reduce the diversity and representativeness of the legislative branch.

Despite these challenges, the qualifications and terms of members of Congress remain an essential component of the U.S. political system, and play a critical role in ensuring that the legislative branch is able to effectively represent the interests and values of the American people.

Powers of Congress, including taxation, commerce, and defense

The U.S. Congress is one of the most powerful legislative bodies in the world, with the authority to make laws and regulations that shape the lives of millions of Americans. Congress is granted these powers by the U.S. Constitution, which outlines the various responsibilities and duties of the legislative branch of government.

One of the most important powers of Congress is the power of taxation. Article I, Section 8 of the Constitution gives Congress the authority to "lay and collect Taxes, Duties, Imposts and Excises, to pay the Debts and provide for the common Defence and general Welfare of the United States." This power allows Congress to raise revenue to fund government programs, national defense, and other essential services. Taxes can take many forms, including income taxes, payroll taxes, and corporate taxes.

Congress also has the power to regulate commerce both within and between states. The Commerce Clause of the Constitution, found in Article I, Section 8, grants Congress the power to "regulate Commerce with foreign Nations, and among the several States, and with the Indian Tribes." This power has been interpreted broadly by the Supreme Court over the years, allowing Congress to regulate a wide range of economic activity, from interstate commerce to environmental regulation.

In addition to taxation and commerce, Congress has the power to declare war and to raise and support armies and navies. This power is critical to the nation's defense and allows Congress to make decisions about national security and foreign policy. Congress also has the power to provide for the common defense, including the power to organize and maintain a militia, as well as to establish rules for the government and regulation of the military.

Other important powers of Congress include the ability to coin money, establish post offices and post roads, and create laws to promote the general welfare of the United States. These powers allow Congress to shape the economic, social, and political landscape of the country.

However, with great power comes great responsibility. Congress must balance its powers with the rights of individual citizens and the need to protect the interests of the nation as a whole. This is not always an easy task, and Congress has faced numerous challenges over the years in attempting to balance competing interests and priorities.

One of the most contentious issues facing Congress in recent years has been the question of healthcare reform. The Affordable Care Act, also known as Obamacare, was passed by Congress in 2010 with the goal of expanding access to healthcare for millions of Americans. However, the law has faced significant opposition from some members of Congress who argue that it represents government overreach and a violation of individual rights. This has led to numerous attempts to repeal or replace the law, as well as legal challenges that have reached the Supreme Court.

Another area of ongoing debate in Congress is immigration policy. With millions of undocumented immigrants living in the United States, Congress has struggled to find a solution that balances the needs of immigrants with the concerns of U.S. citizens. This has led to heated debates over issues such as border security, family separation, and the rights of undocumented immigrants.

Despite these challenges, the powers of Congress remain a critical component of the U.S. government. Through its ability to tax, regulate commerce, and provide for the common defense, Congress has the power to shape the future of the nation and improve the lives of millions of Americans. While there will always be disagreements and competing interests, the ability of Congress to find common ground and work together to achieve common goals remains a hallmark of American democracy.

Procedures for passing laws

In this section, we will explore the procedures and steps involved in passing laws in Congress. From the introduction of a bill to its final passage, there are a number of important stages in the legislative process that are essential to creating effective laws that serve the needs of the American people.

The Constitution for Politicians

At the heart of the legislative process is the concept of democracy, in which elected representatives work to create laws that reflect the will of the people they serve. While the process can be complex and challenging, it is designed to ensure that all voices are heard and that the final result is a law that is fair, just, and beneficial to society as a whole.

The first step in passing a law is the introduction of a bill. Bills can be introduced by any member of Congress, but they must be approved by the appropriate committee before they can be considered by the full House of Representatives or Senate. The committee process is a crucial step in the legislative process, as it allows for detailed analysis and discussion of the bill's contents, as well as input from experts and stakeholders.

Once a bill has been approved by the appropriate committee, it is brought to the floor of the House of Representatives or Senate for debate and voting. During this stage, members of Congress can offer amendments and engage in robust debate about the merits and flaws of the bill. In order for a bill to pass, it must receive a majority of votes in both the House and the Senate.

If a bill is passed by both the House and the Senate, it is sent to a conference committee to reconcile any differences between the two versions of the bill. Once the conference committee has reached a compromise, the bill is sent back to the House and Senate for a final vote. If the bill is passed by both chambers, it is sent to the President for signature or veto.

The process of passing a law can be complex and challenging, and it requires a high level of skill and expertise on the part of members of Congress. However, it is essential to ensuring that the laws of the land reflect the needs and desires of the American people, and that they are designed to promote justice, equality, and the common good.

One important aspect of the legislative process is the role of interest groups and other stakeholders. These groups can play an important role in shaping the content of bills and influencing the legislative process, but they can also create challenges and obstacles to passing laws that are in the best interests of the American people.

In recent years, there has been growing concern about the influence of money in politics, and its impact on the legislative process. Lobbyists and other interest groups have been accused of using their financial resources to influence the votes of members of Congress, and to shape the content of bills in ways that benefit their own interests at the expense of the general public.

Despite these challenges, the legislative process remains an essential part of American democracy, and it is vital that all members of Congress remain committed to upholding the principles of fairness, justice, and the common good. By working together to pass effective laws that serve the needs of the American people, we can continue to build a stronger and more prosperous society for all.

Checks and balances on Congress

The U.S. Constitution is founded on the principle of the separation of powers, which divides the responsibilities of government among three branches: the legislative, executive, and judicial branches. This system of checks and balances is designed to prevent any one branch from becoming too powerful and potentially abusing its authority. Within this framework, Congress is granted significant powers, but it is also subject to a number of checks and balances that limit its authority.

One of the most important checks on Congress is the power of the president to veto legislation. If Congress passes a bill and the president disagrees with it, he or she can veto the bill and send it back to Congress with a message explaining the reasons for the veto. Congress can override a presidential veto with a two-thirds majority vote in both the House of Representatives and the Senate, but this is difficult to achieve in practice. As a result, the president's veto power gives him or her significant leverage in the legislative process and ensures that Congress cannot pass laws that are opposed by the executive branch.

Another check on Congress is the power of the judiciary to review and strike down laws that are deemed unconstitutional. The U.S. Supreme Court has the final say on the meaning and interpretation of the Constitution, and it can declare any law passed by Congress to be unconstitutional and therefore null and void. This power of judicial review is a crucial component of the checks and balances system, as it ensures that Congress does not overstep its constitutional authority.

In addition to these formal checks on Congress, there are also a number of informal checks and balances that help to limit the power of the legislative branch. One such check is the media, which has the power to shine a light on the actions of Congress and hold lawmakers accountable for their actions. By reporting on congressional proceedings and investigating instances of corruption or malfeasance, the media can help to keep Congress in check and ensure that lawmakers are acting in the best interests of their constituents.

Interest groups and advocacy organizations also play an important role in checking the power of Congress. By mobilizing public opinion and lobbying lawmakers on particular issues, these groups can influence the legislative process and ensure that Congress is held accountable to the interests of the people it serves. However, it is worth noting that interest groups and lobbyists can also have a corrupting influence on the legislative process, as lawmakers may be tempted to act in the interests of their donors rather than their constituents.

Finally, the Constitution itself provides a number of checks and balances on the power of Congress. For example, the Bill of Rights protects individual liberties and limits the government's power to infringe upon them. The 10th Amendment reserves certain powers to the states, which can act as a check on federal power. And the constitutional amendment process provides a mechanism for changing the Constitution in response to changing circumstances or social norms.

In conclusion, the power of Congress is subject to a number of checks and balances that help to ensure that it acts in the best interests of the American people. These checks come in many forms, including the president's veto power, judicial review, the media, interest groups, and the Constitution itself. By limiting the power of Congress and ensuring that it acts within the bounds of the Constitution, these checks and balances help to preserve the integrity of the U.S. system of government and protect the rights and liberties of the American people.

Impeachment of federal officials

Impeachment is a unique power of Congress that serves as a check on the executive and judicial branches of the federal government. It allows Congress to remove federal officials from office if they are found to have committed "high crimes and misdemeanors." While the process is relatively rare, it has been used several times throughout American history, most notably during the impeachments of Presidents Andrew Johnson and Bill Clinton.

The Constitution lays out the process for impeachment in Article II, Section 4, which states that "The President, Vice President and all civil Officers of the United States, shall be removed from Office on Impeachment for, and Conviction of, Treason, Bribery, or other high Crimes and Misdemeanors." This means that the House of Representatives has the power to impeach federal officials, while the Senate has the power to hold a trial and remove them from office.

The impeachment process begins in the House of Representatives, where articles of impeachment are introduced by one or more members of the House. The articles of impeachment are essentially a list of charges against the official being impeached, and they must be approved by a simple majority vote of the House. Once the articles of impeachment are approved, the official is considered impeached, which means that they are charged with the crimes or misconduct listed in the articles.

After the official is impeached, the Senate holds a trial to determine whether or not to remove them from office. The trial is presided over by the Chief Justice of the Supreme Court, and the Senate serves as the jury. The official being impeached has the right to a defense, and both sides are allowed to call witnesses and present evidence. A two-thirds majority vote of the Senate is required to remove the official from office.

While impeachment is a powerful tool for holding federal officials accountable, it is not always successful. In fact, only two presidents have ever been impeached: Andrew Johnson in 1868 and Bill Clinton in 1998. Both were ultimately acquitted by the Senate and remained in office. President Richard Nixon was also facing impeachment in 1974, but he resigned before the House could vote on articles of impeachment.

In recent years, impeachment has become a more frequent topic of discussion in American politics. In 2019, President Donald Trump was impeached by the House of Representatives for abuse of power and obstruction of Congress, but he was ultimately acquitted by the Senate. The impeachment of Supreme Court Justice Brett Kavanaugh was also discussed by some members of Congress in 2019, but it did not result in any formal charges.

The use of impeachment as a political tool has led to some controversy and criticism. Some argue that it is being used too frequently and for political purposes, rather than for genuine misconduct or crimes. Others argue that impeachment is an essential tool for holding officials accountable, particularly in cases where they have committed serious offenses.

Overall, the impeachment process serves as a critical check on the power of federal officials and ensures that they are held accountable for their actions. While it can be a contentious and challenging process, it is an essential part of the American system of government and a vital tool for maintaining a balance of power between the executive, legislative, and judicial branches.

Humorous anecdotes about past and present lawmakers

The Constitution for Politicians

Humor has always been a part of politics, and there are plenty of humorous anecdotes about past and present lawmakers that can provide a bit of levity to the often serious business of government. Here are some examples:

The time Rep. Hank Johnson expressed concern about Guam tipping over: In 2010, during a House Armed Services Committee hearing on the impact of military presence on the island of Guam, Rep. Hank Johnson of Georgia expressed concern that the island might become so overpopulated that it would "tip over and capsize." Although his remarks were met with laughter and ridicule at the time, he later clarified that he was using the analogy to express his concerns about the island's infrastructure.

The time Rep. Anthony Weiner accidentally tweeted a lewd photo: In 2011, Rep. Anthony Weiner of New York accidentally tweeted a lewd photo of himself to his followers instead of sending it as a direct message. The scandal led to his resignation from Congress and became a punchline for late-night comedians for months.

The time Sen. Strom Thurmond filibustered for 24 hours: In 1957, Sen. Strom Thurmond of South Carolina set the record for the longest filibuster in Senate history when he spoke for 24 hours and 18 minutes in an attempt to block civil rights legislation. According to legend, he used a steam radiator in the Senate chamber to keep himself hydrated during the marathon speech.

The time Rep. William L. Scott accidentally ate a microphone: In 1968, Rep. William L. Scott of Virginia was addressing the House of Representatives when he accidentally ate part of his microphone. The incident was caught on camera and became a viral sensation, with many people speculating that he had mistaken the microphone for a candy bar.

The time Sen. Al Franken drew a map of the United States: During a 2009 Senate hearing on telecommunications, Sen. Al Franken of Minnesota drew a map of the United States from memory and used it to quiz the CEO of Comcast on the company's coverage areas. The incident showed that even lawmakers can have some fun with their work.

These are just a few examples of the many humorous anecdotes that exist about lawmakers. While politics can be serious business, it's important to remember that lawmakers are human beings who sometimes make mistakes or do silly things. A bit of humor can help to lighten the mood and make the political process a little more enjoyable for everyone involved.

CHAPTER 3: ARTICLE II - THE EXECUTIVE BRANCH

❖   Article II - The Executive Branch
❖   The break down
❖   Powers and responsibilities of the President, including Commander in Chief and head of state
❖   The Vice President's role in government

The Constitution for Politicians

❖ Qualifications and term limits for the President and Vice President
❖ Electoral College and procedures for presidential elections
❖ Powers of the executive branch, including foreign policy and the enforcement of laws
❖ Impeachment of the President
❖ Funny stories about past presidents and their quirks

Article II of the United States Constitution establishes the executive branch of government and outlines the powers and responsibilities of the President and Vice President. It is an essential component of the Constitution, as it ensures that the country is led by qualified individuals who are accountable to the people they serve. In this chapter, we will delve into the various aspects of Article II, including the qualifications and term limits for the President and Vice President, the role of the Vice President in government, and the procedures for presidential elections.

We will also explore the powers of the executive branch, including the President's role as Commander in Chief and head of state, foreign policy, and the enforcement of laws. Finally, we will touch on the controversial topic of impeachment and some funny stories about past presidents and their quirks.

Article II - The Executive Branch

Article II of the United States Constitution establishes the Executive Branch of the federal government, which is responsible for carrying out and enforcing the laws passed by Congress. This branch is headed by the President of the United States, who serves as both the head of state and the head of government. The Vice President, along with the President's Cabinet and various executive departments and agencies, assist the President in carrying out these duties.

Article II outlines the powers and responsibilities of the President, including the ability to sign or veto legislation passed by Congress, negotiate treaties with foreign governments, serve as commander-in-chief of the military, and nominate federal judges and other officials. The President is also responsible for executing the laws of the land and ensuring that the federal government operates effectively and efficiently.

To prevent abuses of power, Article II also establishes various checks and balances on the President. For example, the Senate must approve all presidential appointments, including Supreme Court justices, and Congress has the power to impeach and remove the President for high crimes and misdemeanors.

Additionally, the President is subject to judicial review by the federal courts, which can declare executive actions unconstitutional.

The break down

Article II is all about the Executive Branch of the federal government. This branch is in charge of carrying out and enforcing the laws that Congress passes. The head of this branch is the President of the United States. The Vice President and other important people like the President's Cabinet and different government departments and agencies help the President do his job.

Article II talks about what the President can do and what he's responsible for. The President can sign laws that Congress passes to make them official, or he can say no and veto them. He can also talk with other countries and make agreements called treaties. The President is also the boss of the military and can tell them what to do. He can choose judges and other important people to work for the government too. The President has to make sure that everything the government does is working well.

To make sure the President doesn't have too much power, there are some rules in Article II to keep things in check. For example, the Senate has to say yes before the President can hire anyone for certain jobs. Congress can also get rid of the President if he does something really bad. Finally, the federal courts can say if something the President does isn't allowed by the Constitution.

For Students:

Article II is part of the United States Constitution, which is like a big rulebook for our country. It talks about the Executive Branch, which is the part of the government that is in charge of making sure the laws that Congress passes actually get carried out.

At the head of the Executive Branch is the President of the United States. The President is kind of like the boss of the government. The Vice President and other important people called the Cabinet help the President do his job.

The President has a lot of important jobs to do, like making sure the military is ready to protect our country, signing or saying no to laws that Congress passes, and picking people to work in important government jobs.

But the Constitution also makes sure that the President doesn't have too much power. Other people, like the Senate, have to agree with the President's choices for important jobs. And if the President does something really wrong, like breaking the law, Congress can decide to get rid of him.

So, the Executive Branch is like the part of the government that makes sure everything runs smoothly, but there are rules to make sure nobody gets too powerful.

Powers and responsibilities of the President, including Commander in Chief and head of state

The President of the United States holds a critical role as the head of state and commander-in-chief of the armed forces. As such, the President has numerous powers and responsibilities, including those related to national security, foreign policy, and the enforcement of domestic laws. This chapter will explore the various powers and responsibilities of the President, including those related to national security and military command.

One of the most important roles of the President is that of commander-in-chief of the United States armed forces. In this capacity, the President has the power to direct military operations and make critical decisions related to national security. The President also has the authority to declare war, although this power is often shared with Congress. The President can order troops into combat without a formal declaration of war under certain circumstances, such as in response to an attack on the United States or its interests.

The President is also responsible for the appointment of top military officials, including the Secretary of Defense, the Chairman of the Joint Chiefs of Staff, and other key members of the national security team. The President relies on the advice and expertise of these officials to make informed decisions about military strategy and policy.

As head of state, the President represents the United States on the world stage and serves as a symbol of American values and principles. The President is responsible for foreign policy and diplomacy, including the negotiation of treaties and agreements with other nations. The President also has the authority to appoint ambassadors and other officials who represent the United States in foreign countries.

The President's foreign policy decisions are guided by a number of factors, including national security interests, economic considerations, and humanitarian concerns. The President also works closely with Congress to develop and implement foreign policy initiatives, such as economic sanctions or military aid to foreign allies.

The President's role as head of state also includes ceremonial duties, such as hosting foreign leaders at the White House and participating in diplomatic events around the world. These duties help to strengthen relationships between the United States and other nations and promote goodwill and cooperation on the global stage.

In addition to these responsibilities, the President has a number of other important powers and duties. One of these is the power to sign or veto legislation passed by Congress. If the President signs a bill into law, it becomes part of the United States Code and is enforceable by the federal government. If the President vetoes a bill, it can still become law if two-thirds of both the House of Representatives and the Senate vote to override the veto.

The President is also responsible for the nomination of federal judges and other officials, including members of the Cabinet and the heads of executive agencies. These nominations must be approved by the Senate before the individuals can take office.

Another key responsibility of the President is to execute the laws of the United States and ensure that the federal government operates effectively and efficiently. This includes overseeing the federal bureaucracy and managing the budget and resources of the executive branch.

To assist in these duties, the President relies on the Cabinet and various executive departments and agencies. The Cabinet is composed of the heads of 15 executive departments, including the Department of State, the Department of Defense, and the Department of Justice. The President appoints these officials, who are then subject to Senate confirmation.

The President also has the power to issue executive orders, which are directives that have the force of law but do not require approval by Congress. Executive orders are often used to implement policies or programs that the President believes are necessary for the public good.

Despite the significant powers and responsibilities of the President, the Constitution also establishes various checks and balances to prevent abuses of power. For example, the President is subject to impeachment and removal from office for high crimes and misdemeanors. This process is overseen by Congress and requires a two-thirds vote of the Senate for conviction.

The President is also subject to judicial review by the federal courts, The President is also subject to judicial review by the federal courts, which can declare executive actions unconstitutional. This means that if the President takes an action that goes against the Constitution or the law, the courts can step in and declare that action invalid.

One of the most important powers of the President is his role as Commander-in-Chief of the military. This means that the President is responsible for overseeing and directing the armed forces of the United States. The President can order military action to protect the country or its interests, but he cannot declare war without the approval of Congress. The President also has the power to make treaties with foreign governments, although these treaties must be approved by the Senate.

As head of state, the President represents the United States both at home and abroad. The President welcomes foreign leaders to the United States and attends important international events. The President also has the power to negotiate and sign treaties with foreign governments on behalf of the United States.

The President's responsibilities as head of state also include making sure that the laws of the United States are enforced. The President is responsible for appointing federal judges and other officials, as well as overseeing the activities of executive departments and agencies. The President has the power to issue executive orders, which are directives that carry the force of law. Executive orders can be used to manage the operations of the federal government, and they can also be used to make policy changes without the approval of Congress.

The President's powers and responsibilities are not unlimited, however. The Constitution establishes a system of checks and balances to prevent any one branch of government from becoming too powerful. Congress has the power to impeach and remove the President from office for high crimes and misdemeanors. The Supreme Court can declare executive actions unconstitutional and can strike down laws passed by Congress if they are found to be in violation of the Constitution.

Overall, the President's powers and responsibilities are extensive and far-reaching. The President is responsible for carrying out and enforcing the laws passed by Congress, overseeing the operations of the federal government, and representing the United States both at home and abroad. The President is also subject to checks and balances to prevent abuses of power, ensuring that the United States remains a government of the people, by the people, and for the people.

The Vice President's role in government

The Vice President of the United States is the second-highest-ranking official in the federal government, after the President. The Vice President's role in government is multifaceted and has evolved over time. In this chapter, we will explore the powers and responsibilities of the Vice President, as well as the historical significance of the position.

The Vice President's primary duty is to serve as the first in line of succession to the presidency. In the event that the President is unable to fulfill their duties, either temporarily or permanently, the Vice President assumes the role of President. This has occurred several times throughout American history, most notably when Vice President Lyndon B. Johnson assumed the presidency following the assassination of President John F. Kennedy in 1963.

Beyond serving as a backup to the President, the Vice President also has a number of other responsibilities. One of the Vice President's most important roles is to preside over the Senate. In this capacity, the Vice President is responsible for ensuring that the Senate operates effectively and efficiently. They also have the power to cast a tie-breaking vote in the Senate, which can be crucial in ensuring that important legislation passes.

In addition to presiding over the Senate, the Vice President also has an important role in advising the President. The Vice President serves as a close confidant to the President, and they are often consulted on important policy decisions. In some cases, the Vice President may also be asked to represent the President at diplomatic events or meetings with foreign leaders.

Another important responsibility of the Vice President is to act as a spokesperson for the administration. In this capacity, the Vice President may give speeches or hold press conferences to communicate the President's message to the American people. They may also be called upon to defend the administration's policies or respond to criticism from the opposition party or the media.

The Vice President also has a number of ceremonial duties. They may attend state funerals or other important events on behalf of the President, or represent the United States at international events. In addition, the Vice President often participates in public events and other activities that promote the administration's agenda.

While the Vice President's role in government is primarily supportive, they do have some independent powers and responsibilities. For example, the Vice President has the power to break a tie in the Senate. They also have the power to invoke the 25th Amendment to the Constitution, which allows the Vice President and a majority of the Cabinet to remove the President from office if they are deemed unable to fulfill their duties.

Despite their important role in government, the Vice President has historically been overshadowed by the President. Until the mid-20th century, the Vice President was often seen as a figurehead with little real power or influence. However, in recent decades, the Vice President's role has become more prominent. Vice Presidents have taken on increasingly important roles in advising the President and shaping policy, and their visibility and influence have increased accordingly.

In conclusion, the Vice President of the United States is an important figure in American government, with a range of responsibilities that support the President and promote the administration's agenda. From presiding over the Senate to advising the President and representing the United States on the world stage, the Vice President plays a crucial role in ensuring that the federal government operates effectively and efficiently. While they may not wield as much power as the President, the Vice President's role in government is nevertheless an essential part of the American political system.

Qualifications and term limits for the President and Vice President

The Constitution for Politicians

Qualifications and term limits for the President and Vice President are an important aspect of the United States political system. These requirements help to ensure that those holding the highest offices in the land are qualified and capable of carrying out their responsibilities in an effective and responsible manner. In this chapter, we will explore the qualifications and term limits for the President and Vice President, as well as their historical development and significance.

Qualifications for the President

Article II, Section 1 of the Constitution outlines the qualifications for the presidency. To be eligible for the office of President, an individual must be a natural-born citizen of the United States, at least 35 years old, and have been a resident of the United States for at least 14 years. These qualifications were designed to ensure that the President has a deep understanding of the country and its laws, and that they have a vested interest in the well-being of the nation.

In addition to these formal qualifications, there are also certain characteristics and skills that are often considered important for a successful President. These include strong leadership skills, the ability to communicate effectively with the public and foreign leaders, the ability to make tough decisions under pressure, and a deep understanding of domestic and international issues.

Term Limits for the President

The Constitution also outlines term limits for the President. A President may serve a maximum of two terms in office, with each term lasting four years. This was established by the 22nd Amendment to the Constitution, which was ratified in 1951. Prior to the ratification of the 22nd Amendment, there were no formal term limits for the President, and some Presidents served more than two terms.

The establishment of term limits was a response to concerns about the accumulation of power in the executive branch and the potential for abuse of power by long-serving Presidents. By limiting the number of terms that a President can serve, the Constitution ensures that the office of the President remains fresh and responsive to the needs and desires of the American people.

Qualifications for the Vice President

The qualifications for the Vice President are less strict than those for the President. To be eligible for the office of Vice President, an individual must meet the same citizenship and residency requirements as the President. However, there is no requirement that the Vice President be a natural-born citizen, as there is for the President.

In addition to these formal qualifications, there are also certain characteristics and skills that are often considered important for a successful Vice President. These include the ability to work well with the President, strong communication and interpersonal skills, and a deep understanding of domestic and international issues.

Term Limits for the Vice President

There are no formal term limits for the Vice President. Unlike the President, the Vice President may serve an unlimited number of terms in office. However, the Vice President is subject to the same succession rules as the President, meaning that if the President dies, resigns, or is removed from office, the Vice President assumes the presidency.

The Importance of Qualifications and Term Limits

The qualifications and term limits for the President and Vice President are important for several reasons. First, they help to ensure that those holding these offices are qualified and capable of carrying out their responsibilities in an effective and responsible manner. By establishing minimum age, citizenship, and residency requirements, the Constitution ensures that the President and Vice President have a deep understanding of the country and its laws, and that they have a vested interest in the well-being of the nation.

Second, term limits help to prevent the accumulation of power in the executive branch and the potential for abuse of power by long-serving Presidents. By limiting the number of terms that a President can serve, the Constitution ensures that the office of the President remains fresh and responsive to the needs and desires of the American people.

Third, the qualifications and term limits for the President and Vice President help to ensure that the country is led by qualified individuals and prevent the concentration of power in a single individual or party.

Qualifications for President and Vice President

The Constitution outlines the qualifications for both the President and Vice President. To be eligible to run for President or Vice President, a person must be a natural-born citizen of the United States, at least 35 years old, and have been a resident of the country for at least 14 years. These requirements are meant to ensure that the President and Vice President have a strong connection to the United States and are experienced enough to handle the responsibilities of the office.

Term Limits for President and Vice President

The Constitution also sets term limits for the President and Vice President. The President is limited to two four-year terms, or a maximum of ten years if they serve two years or less of another President's term. This ensures that no single individual can hold the office of President for too long and become too powerful. The 22nd Amendment to the Constitution established this term limit in 1951, after President Franklin D. Roosevelt was elected to four terms.

The Vice President, on the other hand, is not limited to a specific number of terms. However, the Vice President can only serve as President for a maximum of two terms if they were to assume the office of President due to the death, resignation, or impeachment of the previous President.

The 25th Amendment to the Constitution, ratified in 1967, also outlines the procedure for replacing the President and Vice President in case of their death, resignation, or removal from office. The Vice President becomes President if the President is unable to serve, and the President can nominate a new Vice President, subject to the approval of both houses of Congress.

Rationale for Qualifications and Term Limits

The qualifications and term limits for the President and Vice President are essential components of the Constitution that ensure that the country is led by experienced, qualified individuals who are held accountable to the people they serve. These provisions also prevent the accumulation of too much power in a single individual or party, which could lead to tyranny or corruption.

The idea of term limits for the President and Vice President dates back to the era of the founding fathers. During the Constitutional Convention, many delegates were concerned about the possibility of a President serving for life, as was the case with many European monarchs. They believed that term limits were necessary to prevent such a scenario and to ensure that the country was governed by a democratically elected leader.

Term limits also prevent incumbents from becoming too entrenched in their positions and limit their ability to use the office to their personal advantage. Without term limits, a President or Vice President might be tempted to use their power to perpetuate their hold on the office or to enrich themselves and their allies. Term limits ensure that the office remains open to fresh ideas and new leaders, who can bring new perspectives and approaches to governing.

The qualifications for the President and Vice President are also essential to ensure that these individuals have the necessary experience, knowledge, and connection to the country to serve effectively. The natural-born citizen requirement ensures that the President and Vice President have a strong connection to the United

States and a deep understanding of its history and culture. The age and residency requirements ensure that the President and Vice President have the necessary experience and maturity to handle the responsibilities of the office.

Moreover, these qualifications ensure that the President and Vice President are accountable to the people they serve. They are elected by the people through a democratic process, and the people have the power to remove them from office if they do not meet their expectations.

Conclusion

The qualifications and term limits for the President and Vice President are essential components of the Constitution that ensure that the country is led by qualified individuals who are accountable to the people they serve. They prevent the concentration of power in a single individual or office, and promote stability and continuity in government. Additionally, they demonstrate the founders' commitment to democracy and the principle of popular sovereignty.

While there have been debates over the years about the necessity and effectiveness of these qualifications and term limits, they remain a critical aspect of American democracy. They protect against abuses of power, ensure that leadership positions are filled by individuals who are experienced and qualified, and promote a healthy turnover of leadership that allows for new ideas and perspectives to enter government.

Overall, the qualifications and term limits for the President and Vice President serve as important safeguards against the abuse of power and ensure that the United States remains a democratic republic. They are an integral part of the Constitution, and their continued enforcement is crucial for the preservation of American democracy.

The Constitution for Politicians

Electoral College and procedures for presidential elections

The process of electing the President of the United States is a complex one, involving the Electoral College and various procedures that have evolved over the years. The Electoral College is a body of electors appointed by each state to vote for the President and Vice President of the United States. The procedures for presidential elections include everything from the selection of candidates to the counting of votes and the certification of the election results.

The Electoral College

The Electoral College was established by the United States Constitution as a way to select the President and Vice President of the United States. The system was created in part to address concerns about direct democracy and to balance the interests of smaller and larger states. Under this system, each state is assigned a number of electors equal to the combined number of its Senators and Representatives in Congress. For example, California has 55 electors, while Wyoming has only three.

The electors are chosen by the political parties in each state and are typically party activists, local officials, or other individuals who are loyal to the party. In most states, the candidate who wins the popular vote in the state receives all of the state's electors. However, in a few states, the electors are allocated proportionally based on the popular vote. The electors meet in their respective states on the Monday after the second Wednesday in December to cast their votes for President and Vice President.

The procedures for presidential elections

The procedures for presidential elections include everything from the selection of candidates to the counting of votes and the certification of the election results. The process typically begins with the selection of candidates by the political parties. The candidates are chosen through a combination of primaries, caucuses, and conventions. Primaries and caucuses are used to select delegates who will attend the party conventions, where the candidates are officially nominated.

The presidential campaign officially begins on the day after the party conventions and runs until the day of the election. During this time, the candidates travel the country, give speeches, and participate in debates. They also raise money to fund their campaigns and work to build support among voters.

Election Day is held on the Tuesday following the first Monday in November. The polls are open from early in the morning until late in the evening, and voters are required to show identification in order to vote. In most states, voters cast their ballots on paper or using electronic voting machines.

After the polls close, the votes are counted and the results are reported to the state authorities. In some states, the results are reported on the night of the election, while in others, it may take several days or even weeks to count all of the votes. Once the votes are counted, the results are certified by the state authorities and sent to the federal government.

If no candidate receives a majority of the electoral votes (270 out of 538), the election is decided by the House of Representatives. Each state delegation in the House of Representatives is given one vote, and the candidate who receives a majority of the votes in the House is declared the winner.

Controversies and challenges to the electoral process

While the procedures for presidential elections have worked relatively smoothly for most of the country's history, there have been controversies and challenges to the electoral process over the years. One of the most controversial aspects of the Electoral College is the possibility that a candidate could win the popular vote but lose the election. This has happened several times in American history, most recently in the 2016 election, when Donald Trump won the electoral vote but lost the popular vote to Hillary Clinton.

Another controversy that has emerged in recent years is the issue of voter suppression. Some states have passed laws that make it more difficult for certain groups of people, such as minorities and the elderly, to vote. These laws have been challenged in court

Powers of the executive branch, including foreign policy and the enforcement of laws
Impeachment of the President
Funny stories about past presidents and their quirks, with some being struck down as unconstitutional. However, the issue of voter suppression remains a contentious issue in American politics.

Overall, the electoral college and the procedures for presidential elections play a crucial role in American democracy. While there have been controversies and debates surrounding their effectiveness and fairness, they remain a cornerstone of the American political system. By ensuring that every state has a say in the presidential election and that the winner has broad support across the country, the electoral college helps to ensure a peaceful transfer of power and maintains the stability of the American political system.

For Students

So, every four years, people in the United States vote for who they want to be the next president. But the president is not actually chosen directly by the people - instead, we use something called the Electoral College.

The Electoral College is made up of people called electors. Each state gets a certain number of electors based on how many members of Congress they have - this means that bigger states have more electors than smaller states. For example, California has 55 electors, while Wyoming only has 3.

On Election Day, people in each state go to the polls to cast their votes for president. But they're not actually voting directly for the president - instead, they're voting for their state's electors. Each state has a group of electors who are pledged to vote for the candidate who wins the most votes in that state. So if a candidate wins the most votes in California, all of California's 55 electors will vote for that candidate.

The candidate who gets the most electoral votes - not the most popular votes - wins the presidential election. This means that a candidate could win the popular vote - or the most votes from individual people - but still lose the election if they don't get enough electoral votes.

After the election, the electors meet in their respective states to cast their votes. This usually happens in December. Then, in early January, the votes are counted by Congress, and the candidate who gets the most electoral votes is declared the winner.

There are also rules in place to make sure that the president is chosen fairly. For example, no elector can be a member of Congress, and they can't hold any other government position. And if no candidate gets a majority of the electoral votes, the election is decided by the House of Representatives.

So that's a basic explanation of the Electoral College and the procedures for presidential elections in the United States!

Powers of the executive branch, including foreign policy and the enforcement of laws

Article II of the United States Constitution establishes the Executive Branch of the federal government, which is responsible for carrying out and enforcing the laws passed by Congress. The Executive Branch is led by the President of the United States, who is responsible for executing the laws of the land and ensuring that the federal government operates effectively and efficiently. In this chapter, we will discuss the powers of the Executive Branch, including its role in foreign policy and law enforcement.

Foreign Policy

The President of the United States is responsible for setting foreign policy, which refers to the way that the country interacts with other nations. The President has the power to negotiate treaties with foreign governments, appoint ambassadors, and conduct diplomacy with foreign leaders. The President also serves as the commander-in-chief of the armed forces, which means that he or she has the power to direct military operations abroad.

One of the most important tools that the President has in foreign policy is the use of executive agreements. These are agreements between the President and foreign leaders that do not require Senate approval, unlike treaties. This allows the President to act quickly in response to changing events and to bypass the sometimes lengthy and contentious process of obtaining Senate approval for a treaty.

The President also has the power to impose sanctions on other countries, which are penalties intended to influence their behavior. Sanctions can include trade restrictions, travel bans, and asset freezes. The President can also use military force abroad in response to a threat to national security, but this power is constrained by the War Powers Resolution of 1973, which requires the President to seek Congressional approval for military action beyond a certain time limit.

Law Enforcement

The Executive Branch is responsible for enforcing the laws passed by Congress, which includes the criminal justice system. The President has the power to pardon individuals who have been convicted of federal crimes, and to commute their sentences, which means reducing the length of the sentence.

The President also has the power to appoint federal judges, including Supreme Court justices. These appointments can have a significant impact on the interpretation and application of the law, particularly in cases where the Court is closely divided on an issue.

In addition to these powers, the President has significant discretion in how federal laws are enforced. This includes decisions about which crimes to investigate and prosecute, how to allocate resources to different law enforcement agencies, and how to prioritize different types of crimes. This discretion can have a significant impact on the criminal justice system, particularly when it comes to issues like immigration enforcement and drug policy.

Checks and Balances

While the Executive Branch has significant powers, these powers are constrained by the system of checks and balances established by the Constitution. The President must work with Congress to pass laws, and his or her actions are subject to judicial review by the federal courts. Additionally, the President is subject to oversight by Congress, including the power to impeach and remove the President for high crimes and misdemeanors.

Conclusion

The powers of the Executive Branch, including its role in foreign policy and law enforcement, are essential for ensuring that the federal government operates effectively and efficiently. The President of the United States has significant powers in these areas, but these powers are balanced by the system of checks and balances established by the Constitution. The President must work with Congress and the federal courts to ensure that his or her actions are in line with the Constitution and the will of the American people.

Impeachment of the President

Impeachment is the process by which a government official, including the President of the United States, can be removed from office for committing high crimes and misdemeanors. The process of impeachment is a key check on the power of the executive branch and an important safeguard against abuses of power.

The impeachment process begins in the House of Representatives, where a member of Congress can introduce articles of impeachment against the President. These articles must allege specific charges of misconduct, such as abuse of power or obstruction of justice. If a majority of the House votes in favor of the articles of impeachment, the President is officially impeached.

The next step in the process is a trial in the Senate, where Senators serve as the jury and the Chief Justice of the Supreme Court presides over the proceedings. The President is represented by a defense team and has the opportunity to present evidence and call witnesses. The House of Representatives also presents its case against the President.

If two-thirds of the Senators vote to convict the President on one or more of the articles of impeachment, the President is removed from office and may be barred from holding any future public office. If the President is not convicted, he or she remains in office.

Impeachment is a rare occurrence in U.S. history. Only three Presidents have been impeached: Andrew Johnson in 1868, Bill Clinton in 1998, and Donald Trump in 2019 and 2021. None of these Presidents were convicted and removed from office.

The impeachment process is a critical mechanism for holding the President accountable for wrongdoing and ensuring that the executive branch operates within the bounds of the law. However, it is also a highly political process, with members of Congress often voting along party lines. The decision to impeach and remove a President from office is a weighty one, and it is important that it be undertaken with the utmost seriousness and consideration.

In addition to impeachment, there are other mechanisms by which the executive branch can be held accountable for its actions. These include investigations by Congress or independent agencies, lawsuits in federal court, and public pressure from citizens and advocacy groups. The ultimate goal of these mechanisms is to ensure that the President and other executive officials are held to the highest standards of ethical and legal conduct, and that they are accountable to the American people.

Another mechanism for holding the President accountable for their actions is through the power of impeachment. Impeachment is a process by which Congress can investigate and potentially remove the President from office for "high crimes and misdemeanors." This includes any action that violates the law or the Constitution, such as abuse of power, bribery, or obstruction of justice.

The process of impeachment begins in the House of Representatives, where members can introduce articles of impeachment against the President. These articles must be approved by a majority vote in the House before being sent to the Senate for trial. The Senate then serves as the jury, with the Chief Justice of the Supreme Court presiding over the trial. A two-thirds majority vote in the Senate is required to convict the President and remove them from office.

Only two Presidents in US history have been impeached: Andrew Johnson in 1868 and Bill Clinton in 1998. In both cases, however, the Senate did not vote to remove the President from office. Richard Nixon also faced the possibility of impeachment in 1974, but resigned from office before the House could vote on articles of impeachment.

Impeachment is a rare and serious process that should only be used in cases of serious wrongdoing by the President or other executive officials. It serves as a powerful tool for ensuring that the President is held accountable for their actions and upholding the rule of law in the United States.

In addition to impeachment, there are other mechanisms by which the executive branch can be held accountable for its actions. Congress has the power to conduct investigations into the actions of the President and executive officials, and can use its subpoena power to compel testimony and the production of documents. Independent agencies, such as the Department of Justice, can also conduct investigations and bring charges against executive officials who violate the law.

The Constitution for Politicians

Lawsuits in federal court can also hold the executive branch accountable for its actions. Citizens and advocacy groups can sue the government for violating their rights or for failing to enforce the law. These lawsuits can lead to court orders and injunctions that require the government to change its policies or actions.

Finally, public pressure and activism can also be effective tools for holding the executive branch accountable. Mass protests, social media campaigns, and other forms of activism can draw attention to important issues and put pressure on elected officials to take action. In some cases, public pressure can lead to resignations or changes in policy, even without the need for impeachment or legal action.

Overall, the Constitution and the laws of the United States provide a range of mechanisms for holding the executive branch accountable for its actions. These mechanisms are essential for ensuring that the President and other executive officials are held to the highest standards of ethical and legal conduct, and that they are accountable to the American people.

Impeachment is a process by which the House of Representatives brings charges against a federal official, including the President, for "high crimes and misdemeanors." If the House votes to impeach, the case then moves to the Senate for a trial. If two-thirds of the Senate votes to convict, the official is removed from office. However, there is a scenario in which the President could remain in office even if they are impeached by the House and convicted by the Senate.

If the impeachment and conviction take place during the President's last few days in office, the removal from office would be moot since the President's term would be ending anyway. Additionally, impeachment and conviction do not automatically result in criminal charges or imprisonment. Rather, they are political processes intended to hold federal officials accountable for their actions while in office.

Funny stories about past presidents and their quirks

As much as the presidency is a serious and important job, there have been many humorous and quirky moments throughout the history of the United States. Here are a few funny stories about past presidents and their quirks:

Andrew Jackson's Parrot: Andrew Jackson, the seventh president of the United States, had a pet parrot named Poll. The parrot had a habit of swearing, which Jackson found amusing. Unfortunately, when Jackson died, the parrot had to be removed from his funeral because it wouldn't stop swearing.

William Howard Taft's Bathtub: William Howard Taft, the 27th president of the United States, was known for his large size. Legend has it that he once got stuck in the White House bathtub and had to be helped out by his aides.

Theodore Roosevelt's Love of Animals: Theodore Roosevelt, the 26th president of the United States, was a big fan of animals. He had a collection of pets, including a bear, a badger, a pig, and a macaw. He even took his bear on a walk around the White House grounds.

John Quincy Adams' Skinny-Dipping: John Quincy Adams, the sixth president of the United States, was known for his daily swims in the Potomac River. He was so dedicated to his swimming routine that he often went skinny-dipping.

Calvin Coolidge's Silence: Calvin Coolidge, the 30th president of the United States, was famously quiet. He was known for his terse communication style and for being a man of few words. When a reporter once bet him that he couldn't get Coolidge to say more than two words, Coolidge responded, "You lose."

Richard Nixon's Love of Ketchup: Richard Nixon, the 37th president of the United States, was a big fan of ketchup. He reportedly put it on everything from his eggs to his cottage cheese.

The Constitution for Politicians

Ronald Reagan's Sense of Humor: Ronald Reagan, the 40th president of the United States, was known for his sense of humor. He was particularly fond of telling jokes, both in public and in private. One of his most famous jokes was, "I'm not worried about the deficit. It's big enough to take care of itself."

These are just a few examples of the funny and quirky moments that have occurred throughout the history of the presidency. Despite the seriousness of the job, it's important to remember that presidents are human too and have their own unique personalities and quirks.

Conclusion:

Article II of the Constitution is a critical part of the U.S. government's framework that outlines the responsibilities and limitations of the executive branch. It is designed to prevent the concentration of power in a single individual or entity and ensure that the President and Vice President are held accountable to the American people.

The provisions outlined in Article II have played a significant role in shaping U.S. history and politics, from the procedures for presidential elections to the powers of the executive branch. The Vice President's role in government, as well as the qualifications and term limits for the President and Vice President, have been crucial in ensuring that the country is led by qualified individuals.

The impeachment process and funny stories about past presidents remind us that even the most powerful individuals in government are human and subject to scrutiny and criticism. Overall, Article II serves as a foundation for the U.S. government's structure and principles and remains a vital document for the American people.

The Constitution for Politicians

CHAPTER 4: ARTICLE III - THE JUDICIAL BRANCH

- ❖ Article III - The Judicial Branch
- ❖ The break down
- ❖ Establishment of the Supreme Court and other federal courts
- ❖ The role of the Supreme Court and other federal courts
- ❖ The importance of the judicial system in interpreting laws
- ❖ Jurisdiction and powers of the federal courts
- ❖ Appointment and qualifications of federal judges
- ❖ Interpretation of the Constitution and federal laws
- ❖ Impeachment of federal judges
- ❖ Humorous examples of famous court cases

Chapter 4 of the United States Constitution outlines the establishment and powers of the federal judiciary. The judiciary is a critical branch of the federal government that ensures the protection of individual rights and upholds the Constitution and federal law. The chapter covers the creation of the Supreme Court and other federal courts, the appointment and qualifications of federal judges, the jurisdiction and powers of the federal courts, and the interpretation of the Constitution and federal laws.

Article III - The Judicial Branch

Article III of the United States Constitution establishes the judicial branch of the federal government. It creates the Supreme Court and authorizes Congress to establish lower federal courts. The judicial branch is responsible for interpreting the Constitution and federal laws, as well as resolving disputes between individuals, organizations, and government entities.

The judicial branch serves as a crucial check and balance on the power of the other two branches of government, the legislative and executive branches. It ensures that the laws and actions of these branches are consistent with the Constitution and do not infringe upon individual rights and liberties.

The Constitution grants the judicial branch significant independence from the other branches of government. Judges and justices are appointed for life, subject only to removal through the impeachment process. This provides them with the freedom to interpret the law without fear of political retaliation.

Throughout history, the judicial branch has played a vital role in shaping American society. It has made landmark decisions in cases involving civil rights, voting rights, and other fundamental liberties. The Supreme Court, in particular, has become a key institution in American politics, often serving as the final arbiter of legal disputes and the ultimate protector of individual rights.

Overall, the judicial branch plays a crucial role in maintaining the balance of power within the federal government and ensuring that the rights and liberties of all Americans are protected. In the following sections, we will explore the key components of the judicial branch in more detail.

The break down

The breakdown of Article III of the U.S. Constitution, which outlines the judicial branch of government, can be summarized as follows:

Section 1 establishes the Supreme Court as the highest court in the land, with the authority to hear cases and controversies arising under the Constitution, federal law, and treaties.

Section 2 specifies the jurisdiction of the federal courts, including cases involving ambassadors, public ministers, and consuls, as well as cases in which the United States is a party. It also establishes the right to trial by jury in criminal cases and sets out the definition of treason.

The Constitution for Politicians

Section 3 defines the crime of treason against the United States, which requires the testimony of two witnesses to the same overt act of treason or a confession in open court.

Section 4 guarantees that the United States will have a republican form of government and protects against domestic violence.

Overall, Article III establishes the framework for the federal court system and outlines the responsibilities of the judiciary in interpreting and upholding the Constitution and federal law.

For the students

Article III of the United States Constitution talks about the judicial branch. The judicial branch is responsible for interpreting the law and making sure that the laws are being followed.

There are three important things to know about the judicial branch:

The judicial branch is made up of different kinds of courts. The most important court is the Supreme Court, which is the highest court in the land. The Supreme Court has nine justices who are appointed by the President and confirmed by the Senate.

The judges in the judicial branch serve for life, unless they retire or are impeached. This is because judges need to be independent and not influenced by politics.

The judicial branch is responsible for making sure that the laws and actions of the other branches of government (the legislative and executive branches) are fair and constitutional. This means that if someone thinks that a law is unfair or unconstitutional, they can go to court and ask a judge to decide.

Overall, the judicial branch is important because it helps make sure that the laws and actions of the government are fair and follow the Constitution.

Establishment of the Supreme Court and other federal courts

The establishment of the Supreme Court and other federal courts is an important component of the United States government. Article III of the U.S. Constitution establishes the judicial branch of the government and outlines the powers and responsibilities of the Supreme Court and other federal courts.

The Constitution grants the power to establish and maintain federal courts to the Congress. The first federal court established by Congress was the United States District Court for the District of Pennsylvania, which was created in 1789. Since then, the federal court system has grown to include district courts, circuit courts of appeal, and the Supreme Court.

The district courts are the trial courts of the federal court system. There is at least one district court in each state, and some states are divided into multiple districts. District court judges are appointed by the President and confirmed by the Senate, and they serve for life or until they resign, retire, or are impeached.

The circuit courts of appeal are the intermediate appellate courts of the federal court system. There are thirteen circuit courts, and they hear appeals from the district courts within their geographic jurisdiction. Circuit court judges are also appointed by the President and confirmed by the Senate, and they serve for life or until they resign, retire, or are impeached.

The Supreme Court is the highest court in the federal court system. It is composed of nine justices who are appointed by the President and confirmed by the Senate. The justices serve for life or until they resign, retire, or are impeached. The Supreme Court has the power of judicial review, which means it can declare federal laws or actions unconstitutional.

In addition to the Supreme Court and the lower federal courts, there are also specialized federal courts. These include the Court of Appeals for the Federal Circuit, the Court of International Trade, the Court of Federal Claims, and the Tax Court. These courts have specific jurisdiction over certain types of cases, such as patent disputes or cases involving the federal government.

The establishment of the federal court system is crucial for ensuring that the laws of the United States are interpreted and applied fairly and consistently. The federal courts have the power to resolve disputes between individuals, businesses, and government entities, and to uphold the rights and freedoms guaranteed by the Constitution.

However, the federal court system is not without its challenges. One of the biggest challenges is ensuring that the courts remain independent and free from political influence. Federal judges are appointed by the President and confirmed by the Senate, which means their selection and confirmation can be influenced by political considerations. Additionally, some judges may be tempted to rule in a way that aligns with their personal or political beliefs, rather than the law and the Constitution.

Another challenge facing the federal court system is the backlog of cases. The courts are responsible for resolving an enormous number of cases every year, and the sheer volume of cases can lead to delays in the judicial process. This can be frustrating for individuals and businesses who are waiting for a resolution to their case, and it can also lead to a perception that the courts are slow or inefficient.

Despite these challenges, the federal court system remains an important pillar of the U.S. government. It plays a critical role in interpreting and upholding the laws and the Constitution, and it helps to ensure that justice is served fairly and consistently throughout the country.

The role of the Supreme Court and other federal courts

The role of the Supreme Court and other federal courts is essential in upholding the Constitution and ensuring justice for all Americans. The Constitution established the Supreme Court as the highest court in the land and also authorized Congress to create lower federal courts. Together, these courts interpret and enforce the law, ensuring that our democracy functions as intended.

The Supreme Court is composed of nine justices, who are appointed by the President and confirmed by the Senate. Once appointed, justices serve for life, or until they retire or are removed from the bench. This ensures that the Court can remain independent and impartial, free from political pressures.

The main role of the Supreme Court is to interpret the Constitution and federal laws. When a case comes before the Court, the justices review the arguments and evidence presented by both sides and apply the law to the facts of the case. The Court's decision in each case becomes precedent, or a guiding principle for future cases with similar issues.

The Supreme Court also has the power of judicial review, which allows it to declare acts of Congress or the President unconstitutional. This power was established in the landmark case Marbury v. Madison (1803) and has since been used by the Court to strike down laws and policies that it deems unconstitutional.

In addition to the Supreme Court, there are also lower federal courts, including the district courts and the circuit courts of appeals. District courts are trial courts that hear cases at the federal level, while the circuit courts of appeals hear appeals from the district courts. These courts play a crucial role in the federal judicial system, as they handle the majority of federal cases.

The role of the federal courts goes beyond interpreting and enforcing the law. They also serve as a check on the other branches of government. For example, the courts can strike down laws or policies that violate the Constitution or other federal laws, even if those laws or policies are supported by the President or Congress. In this way, the courts can help to ensure that the government operates within the limits of the law and respects the rights of all Americans.

One of the most important cases in the history of the Supreme Court was Brown v. Board of Education (1954). In this case, the Court declared that segregation in public schools was unconstitutional. This decision paved the way for the Civil Rights Movement and had a profound impact on American society.

Another landmark case was Roe v. Wade (1973), in which the Supreme Court established a woman's right to choose to have an abortion. This decision has been highly controversial and has been the subject of ongoing debate and political controversy.

The Supreme Court also plays an important role in interpreting the Bill of Rights, the first ten amendments to the Constitution. These amendments protect the rights of individuals, such as the right to free speech, the right to bear arms, and the right to a fair trial. Over the years, the Court has issued many important decisions interpreting these rights and balancing them against other interests, such as public safety or national security.

One controversial issue that has come before the Supreme Court in recent years is same-sex marriage. In the landmark case Obergefell v. Hodges (2015), the Court held that the Constitution guarantees the right to marry for same-sex couples. This decision was celebrated by many as a victory for civil rights, but it was also criticized by some who felt that the Court had overstepped its bounds.

The federal courts also play an important role in protecting individual rights and ensuring that justice is served. For example, federal courts have heard cases involving police misconduct, voting rights, and discrimination. Through their decisions, the courts help to shape the course of American society and uphold the values of justice and equality.

The Constitution for Politicians

In addition to their role in interpreting and enforcing the law, the federal courts also play an important role in the administration of justice and in interpreting and enforcing the law, the federal courts also play an important role in the administration of justice. This includes overseeing the criminal justice system and ensuring that individuals accused of crimes are afforded due process of law.

The federal courts have jurisdiction over a wide range of criminal offenses, including those that violate federal law and those that occur on federal property or involve federal officials. They also have the power to hear certain civil cases, such as those involving disputes between citizens of different states or cases involving federal laws and regulations.

One of the most important functions of the federal courts in the administration of justice is to protect individual rights and liberties. This includes interpreting the Constitution and other laws to ensure that they are applied fairly and in accordance with the principles of due process, equal protection, and freedom of speech, religion, and the press.

For example, the Supreme Court has issued landmark decisions that have expanded individual rights and protections, such as Brown v. Board of Education (1954), which struck down racial segregation in public schools, and Roe v. Wade (1973), which established a woman's right to choose to have an abortion.

The federal courts also play a crucial role in protecting civil liberties during times of national crisis. For example, during World War II, the Supreme Court ruled in Korematsu v. United States (1944) that the internment of Japanese Americans was constitutional, but this decision has since been widely criticized as a violation of individual rights.

More recently, the federal courts have played a key role in protecting civil liberties in the post-9/11 era. In cases such as Hamdi v. Rumsfeld (2004) and Boumediene v. Bush (2008), the Supreme Court ruled that individuals detained as "enemy combatants" have the right to challenge their detention in court and to be afforded due process of law.

In addition to their role in protecting individual rights, the federal courts also play a critical role in shaping public policy. This includes interpreting federal laws and regulations, which can have a significant impact on issues such as environmental protection, civil rights, and consumer protection.

For example, the Supreme Court has issued major rulings on issues such as campaign finance (Citizens United v. FEC, 2010), same-sex marriage (Obergefell v. Hodges, 2015), and the Affordable Care Act (NFIB v. Sebelius, 2012).

Overall, the federal courts, and particularly the Supreme Court, play a vital role in shaping the direction of the country and protecting individual rights and liberties. While their decisions are often controversial and subject to debate, their authority and influence in American society is unquestioned.

The importance of the judicial system in interpreting laws

The judicial system plays a crucial role in interpreting and applying laws in the United States. The interpretation of laws is essential to the effective functioning of a democratic society, as it ensures that individuals and institutions are held accountable for their actions and that the rights of citizens are protected.

One of the primary responsibilities of the judicial system is to interpret the Constitution and other laws passed by the legislative branch. The Constitution, which is the supreme law of the land, provides the framework for the government and establishes the rights and protections of citizens. The interpretation of the Constitution has been the subject of many landmark Supreme Court cases, which have shaped the course of American history.

The Constitution for Politicians

For example, in the case of Marbury v. Madison in 1803, the Supreme Court established the principle of judicial review, which gives the Court the power to declare laws unconstitutional if they are found to violate the Constitution. This decision was a critical moment in the development of the American legal system and has had far-reaching implications for the interpretation of laws and the balance of power between the three branches of government.

In addition to interpreting the Constitution, the federal courts also interpret and apply laws passed by Congress and state legislatures. This is an essential function of the judicial system, as it ensures that laws are applied fairly and consistently across the country. For example, in cases involving federal laws, such as civil rights or environmental protection, the federal courts play a crucial role in enforcing these laws and holding individuals and institutions accountable for violations.

Moreover, the federal courts also have a significant impact on the development of the law. Through their decisions, the courts establish legal precedents that guide the interpretation and application of laws in future cases. This process of precedent-setting is critical to the development of a legal system that is fair, consistent, and responsive to the needs of society.

Furthermore, the federal courts also play a vital role in protecting individual rights and liberties. This is especially true for the Supreme Court, which has issued numerous landmark decisions that have expanded the rights and protections of citizens. For example, in the case of Brown v. Board of Education in 1954, the Court struck down racial segregation in public schools, a decision that paved the way for the civil rights movement.

Similarly, in the case of Roe v. Wade in 1973, the Supreme Court established a woman's right to choose to have an abortion, a decision that has been the subject of ongoing controversy and debate. These decisions highlight the critical role that the judicial system plays in protecting the rights and freedoms of individuals in the United States.

Another important function of the judicial system is to resolve disputes between individuals and organizations. This is achieved through the civil court system, which hears cases involving contract disputes, personal injury claims, and other legal issues. The federal courts also play a crucial role in resolving disputes between the federal government and state governments, such as cases involving constitutional issues or disputes over federal laws.

Overall, the judicial system plays a critical role in interpreting laws, protecting individual rights and liberties, and resolving disputes in a fair and impartial manner. The federal courts, in particular, have a significant impact on the development of the law, as their decisions establish legal precedents that guide the interpretation and application of laws in future cases. By upholding the rule of law and ensuring that individuals and institutions are held accountable for their actions, the judicial system serves as a cornerstone of American democracy.

Jurisdiction and powers of the federal courts

The federal courts are an integral part of the judicial system in the United States. Their jurisdiction and powers are outlined in the U.S. Constitution and federal law. Understanding the jurisdiction and powers of the federal courts is essential to understanding how the judicial system works and how it impacts everyday life.

Jurisdiction refers to the authority of a court to hear and decide a case. The federal courts have limited jurisdiction, meaning they can only hear cases that fall within their specified authority. The jurisdiction of the federal courts is determined by both the Constitution and federal statutes.

Article III of the Constitution establishes the judicial branch of government and grants the federal courts jurisdiction over cases involving federal law, the Constitution, and disputes between states. This is known as federal question jurisdiction. In addition, the Constitution gives the federal courts jurisdiction over cases involving foreign governments and diplomats, as well as maritime and admiralty cases.

Federal courts also have diversity jurisdiction, which allows them to hear cases between citizens of different states or between a citizen and a foreign government. Diversity jurisdiction is intended to prevent state bias in lawsuits involving parties from different states or countries.

The jurisdiction of the federal courts is further defined by federal statutes, which outline the types of cases that fall within federal court jurisdiction. For example, the federal courts have jurisdiction over cases involving patents, trademarks, copyrights, antitrust laws, and bankruptcy.

The powers of the federal courts are also outlined in the Constitution and federal law. The most significant power of the federal courts is the power of judicial review, which allows them to declare laws or government actions unconstitutional. This power was established in the landmark case Marbury v. Madison (1803), in which the Supreme Court declared that the Constitution grants the federal courts the power to strike down laws that are contrary to its provisions.

In addition to the power of judicial review, the federal courts have the power to interpret federal law and to enforce it. This includes the power to issue injunctions, which are court orders that require a person or entity to take a certain action or to refrain from taking a certain action. Federal courts also have the power to issue writs, which are orders that compel a government official or agency to perform a specific duty.

Another important power of the federal courts is the power to interpret the Constitution. The Constitution is a living document that has been interpreted in different ways throughout history. The federal courts have the power to interpret the Constitution and to apply its provisions to modern-day issues. This power is critical in protecting individual rights and ensuring that the government operates within the limits set by the Constitution.

The Constitution for Politicians

The federal courts also have the power to adjudicate disputes between the federal government and individual citizens or states. This includes cases involving constitutional challenges to federal laws or regulations, as well as cases involving disputes between states or between states and the federal government.

The Supreme Court, as the highest court in the land, has the ultimate authority to interpret the Constitution and to make final decisions on federal law. The Supreme Court also has the power to review decisions made by lower federal courts and state courts. This power of judicial review is critical in maintaining the balance of power between the three branches of government and in ensuring that the Constitution is upheld.

In conclusion, the jurisdiction and powers of the federal courts are essential to the functioning of the judicial system in the United States. The federal courts have the authority to hear and decide cases that fall within their jurisdiction, as well as the power to interpret and enforce federal law and the Constitution. The Supreme Court, as the highest court in the land, plays a critical role in interpreting the Constitution and making final decisions on federal law. Understanding the jurisdiction and powers of the federal courts is key to understanding the role of the judicial system in upholding the rule of law and protecting individual rights.

Federal courts have the power to decide cases that involve federal law, the Constitution, and disputes between citizens of different states or between citizens and the federal government. This is known as federal question jurisdiction and diversity jurisdiction, respectively. In addition, federal courts have the power of judicial review, which allows them to interpret the Constitution and determine whether actions by the legislative or executive branches are constitutional.

The federal courts also have the power to issue injunctions, or orders that require individuals or entities to stop certain actions or to take certain actions. This power is critical in enforcing federal law and protecting individual rights, as it allows courts to prevent harm from occurring or to require individuals or entities to make amends for harm that has already occurred.

Another important power of the federal courts is the power to hold individuals or entities in contempt of court. This occurs when an individual or entity defies a court order, and can result in fines or even imprisonment.

The federal courts also have the power to appoint and supervise certain court officials, such as bankruptcy trustees and federal public defenders. This helps to ensure that court proceedings are fair and impartial.

It is important to note that the powers of the federal courts are not unlimited. For example, they do not have the power to hear cases that only involve state law, unless the case involves a federal question or diversity jurisdiction. In addition, the Supreme Court can only hear cases that are properly appealed to it and that fall within its jurisdiction.

The jurisdiction and powers of the federal courts have been the subject of much debate and controversy throughout the history of the United States. Critics have argued that federal courts, particularly the Supreme Court, have overstepped their bounds and have taken on roles that should be reserved for the legislative or executive branches. Others argue that the federal courts have an important role to play in upholding the Constitution and protecting individual rights, particularly in cases where other branches of government are not adequately protecting those rights.

Overall, the jurisdiction and powers of the federal courts are a critical component of the judicial system in the United States. They allow federal courts to hear and decide cases that fall within their authority, to interpret and enforce federal law and the Constitution, and to protect individual rights. While there may be debate over the proper role of the federal courts, it is clear that they play an important role in ensuring justice and upholding the rule of law in the United States.

Appointment and qualifications of federal judges

The appointment of federal judges is one of the most important responsibilities of the President of the United States, as it has a significant impact on the interpretation and enforcement of federal law. The qualifications and selection process for federal judges are outlined in the Constitution and subsequent legislation.

Qualifications for federal judges

According to the Constitution, federal judges must be appointed by the President and confirmed by the Senate. In addition, federal judges must meet certain qualifications. Specifically, judges must be at least 18 years old and have good standing in the bar of the state in which they practice law. They must also be a citizen of the United States.

There are no specific requirements for education or experience, although most judges have a law degree and prior experience practicing law or serving as a judge in state courts. In addition, many judges are appointed based on their political affiliations or prior service to the President.

Appointment of federal judges

The President of the United States has the authority to appoint all federal judges, including Supreme Court Justices, with the advice and consent of the Senate. This means that the President must nominate a candidate for the position, and the Senate Judiciary Committee will then hold hearings to evaluate the nominee's qualifications and fitness for the position.

If the committee approves the nomination, it will then be voted on by the full Senate. If the nominee receives a majority of votes, they will be confirmed and officially appointed as a federal judge.

The appointment process for Supreme Court Justices is particularly important, as they serve for life and have significant influence on the interpretation and enforcement of federal law. The President's nominees to the Supreme Court are often scrutinized closely by both political parties and advocacy groups, as they can shape the court's direction for years to come.

Powers and responsibilities of federal judges

Once appointed, federal judges have significant powers and responsibilities in the judicial system. They are responsible for interpreting and applying federal law and the Constitution, and have the authority to make final decisions on legal disputes. This includes both civil and criminal cases, as well as cases involving federal laws and regulations.

In addition, federal judges have the power to issue rulings on constitutional issues, which can have significant implications for the interpretation and enforcement of federal law. For example, in the landmark case Brown v. Board of Education, the Supreme Court ruled that segregation in public schools was unconstitutional, setting the stage for desegregation efforts across the country.

Federal judges also have the authority to issue injunctions and other orders that require individuals or organizations to comply with federal law. This includes orders to stop illegal activities, enforce regulations, or provide relief to individuals or groups that have been harmed by illegal behavior.

Impartiality and ethics of federal judges

One of the most important qualities for a federal judge is impartiality. Judges must be able to put aside their personal beliefs and biases and make decisions based solely on the facts and the law. This is particularly important in cases that involve controversial or politically sensitive issues, where impartiality is essential to maintaining public trust in the judicial system.

In addition, federal judges are subject to strict ethical guidelines and standards. They must avoid conflicts of interest, maintain confidentiality, and conduct themselves in a manner that upholds the integrity and impartiality of the judicial system.

Removal of federal judges

Although federal judges serve for life, they can be removed from office through the process of impeachment. This process is similar to that of the President, with the House of Representatives bringing charges and the Senate holding a trial to determine whether the judge should be removed from office.

However, unlike the President, federal judges can also be removed for reasons of misconduct or incapacity. This process is overseen by the Judicial Council of the relevant circuit or by the Judicial Conference of the United States, and can result in the judge being censured, suspended, or even removed from their position.

Furthermore, there are several qualifications that an individual must possess in order to be considered for appointment as a federal judge. According to Article III of the Constitution, federal judges must be appointed by the President with the advice and consent of the Senate. They hold their office for life, provided they maintain "good behavior." This means that a federal judge can only be removed from office through the process of impeachment, as mentioned earlier.

In terms of qualifications, there are no specific requirements listed in the Constitution for becoming a federal judge. However, in practice, most federal judges have extensive legal experience, often including experience as a lawyer or prosecutor, and many have served as state or federal judges in the past. Additionally, there is often a focus on appointing judges with strong academic credentials, such as those who have graduated from prestigious law schools or have published legal scholarship.

The appointment of federal judges is a highly politicized process, particularly at the level of the Supreme Court. The President typically appoints judges who share their political ideology, and the Senate's approval process often involves a thorough examination of the nominee's past judicial opinions, political views, and personal background. This can result in significant partisan divisions and controversy, particularly when a vacancy arises on the Supreme Court.

There have been several notable moments in history related to the appointment of federal judges. One of the most significant was the confirmation of Clarence Thomas to the Supreme Court in 1991. Thomas faced allegations of sexual harassment during his confirmation hearings, which resulted in a highly contentious process and ultimately led to him being narrowly confirmed by the Senate.

Another important moment in the history of federal judicial appointments was the decision by Senate Republicans in 2016 to refuse to hold hearings or a vote on President Obama's nominee to the Supreme Court, Merrick Garland. This decision was made in the months leading up to the 2016 presidential election, and Republicans argued that the next President should have the opportunity to fill the vacant seat on the Court.

In conclusion, the appointment and qualifications of federal judges play a critical role in the functioning of the judicial system in the United States. Federal judges must possess significant legal experience and often hold strong academic credentials, and their appointment is a highly politicized process. Despite this, federal judges are held to high ethical and professional standards, and their role in interpreting and enforcing the law is essential to upholding the principles of the Constitution and ensuring the fair administration of justice.

Interpretation of the Constitution and federal laws

Interpretation of the Constitution and federal laws is a crucial aspect of the role of the federal courts in the United States. The Constitution and federal laws establish the framework for the nation's government and legal system, and the interpretation of these documents shapes how laws are enforced, how disputes are resolved, and how the rights of citizens are protected.

The Constitution for Politicians

The Constitution, in particular, is the foundation of the legal system in the United States. It establishes the structure of the federal government, outlines the powers of each branch, and sets forth the basic rights of citizens. However, the Constitution is not a detailed guide to every aspect of governance and law, and it leaves many issues open to interpretation.

One of the most important principles of the judicial system in the United States is the concept of judicial review. This principle, which was established in the landmark Supreme Court case Marbury v. Madison in 1803, gives the federal courts the power to review the actions of the other branches of government and determine whether they are constitutional.

The power of judicial review has far-reaching implications for the interpretation of the Constitution and federal laws. It means that the Supreme Court and other federal courts have the authority to strike down laws that are deemed unconstitutional. This power is essential to ensuring that the government operates within the limits of the Constitution and that the rights of citizens are protected.

The interpretation of the Constitution and federal laws is not always straightforward. The language used in these documents is often vague or ambiguous, and different people may have different interpretations of what certain provisions mean. As a result, the federal courts have developed a number of different approaches to interpreting these documents.

One approach to interpreting the Constitution and federal laws is known as originalism. This approach holds that the meaning of the Constitution and federal laws should be interpreted in light of the original intent of the framers. In other words, the courts should look to the historical context in which these documents were written and try to determine what the authors of the documents intended.

Another approach to interpreting the Constitution and federal laws is known as textualism. This approach holds that the meaning of the Constitution and federal laws should be determined based on the plain language of the text. Under this approach, the courts should not look to the historical context or the intentions of the framers, but should instead focus solely on the words used in the document.

A third approach to interpreting the Constitution and federal laws is known as living constitutionalism. This approach holds that the meaning of the Constitution and federal laws should evolve over time to reflect changes in society and technology. Under this approach, the courts may look to the historical context and the intentions of the framers, but they also take into account the changing needs and values of society.

The approach that the federal courts take to interpreting the Constitution and federal laws can have significant implications for the way that laws are enforced and the rights of citizens. For example, the Supreme Court's interpretation of the Second Amendment, which protects the right to bear arms, has been the subject of intense debate in recent years. Some people believe that the Second Amendment guarantees an individual right to own guns, while others believe that it only protects the right to bear arms as part of a well-regulated militia.

The interpretation of federal laws is also an important aspect of the role of the federal courts. When Congress passes a law, it is up to the federal courts to interpret that law and determine how it should be applied. This can be a complex process, as federal laws often interact with state laws and regulations, as well as with other federal laws.

One of the key principles of interpreting federal laws is known as statutory construction. This principle holds that the courts should interpret federal laws in a way that gives effect to the intent of Congress. In other words, the courts should try to determine what Congress meant when it passed a particular law and apply that meaning to the case at hand. This can involve looking at the text of the law itself, as well as its legislative history, which includes committee reports, floor debates, and other materials related to the law's passage.

Another important principle in interpreting federal laws is known as stare decisis, which means "let the decision stand." This principle holds that courts should generally follow the precedent established by previous court decisions, particularly those from higher courts. This helps to promote consistency and predictability in the application of the law.

In addition to interpreting federal laws, the federal courts also play a critical role in interpreting the Constitution. The Constitution is the supreme law of the land, and all federal and state laws must be consistent with its provisions. When a case raises a constitutional issue, the federal courts must interpret the Constitution and determine whether the law in question is constitutional.

The Supreme Court, in particular, has played a pivotal role in interpreting the Constitution throughout American history. Some of the Court's most famous cases involve constitutional issues, such as Brown v. Board of Education, which declared segregation in public schools to be unconstitutional, and Roe v. Wade, which established a woman's right to an abortion.

In interpreting the Constitution, the federal courts use several different approaches. One of the most widely used is known as originalism, which holds that the Constitution should be interpreted according to its original meaning at the time it was adopted. This approach emphasizes the importance of the text of the Constitution, as well as the historical context in which it was written.

Another approach to constitutional interpretation is known as living constitutionalism, which holds that the Constitution should be interpreted in light of changing social and political circumstances. This approach emphasizes the need for the Constitution to remain relevant and adaptable to modern times.

Regardless of the approach used, the interpretation of federal laws and the Constitution is a critical function of the federal courts. It ensures that laws are applied fairly and consistently, and that the rights of all individuals are protected under the law.

However, the interpretation of federal laws and the Constitution is not always straightforward. There can be disagreements among judges and legal scholars about the meaning of particular provisions, and the courts must navigate complex legal and social issues in order to make their decisions.

Furthermore, the interpretation of federal laws and the Constitution can have far-reaching consequences for individuals and society as a whole. Court decisions can impact the lives of millions of people, and can have significant political and economic implications.

As such, the interpretation of federal laws and the Constitution is a weighty responsibility, and one that requires judges to approach their work with care, diligence, and a commitment to upholding the principles of justice and the rule of law. It is a critical aspect of the federal judicial system, and one that ensures that the United States remains a nation governed by laws and not by arbitrary power.

Impeachment of federal judges

The process of impeachment is not limited to the President of the United States; it also applies to federal judges. In fact, there have been several instances throughout American history where federal judges have been impeached and removed from office. This chapter will explore the process of impeaching federal judges and some of the notable cases where it has been employed.

The Constitution grants Congress the power to remove federal judges through the process of impeachment. Article II, Section 4 states that federal judges, including Supreme Court justices, can be impeached for "high crimes and misdemeanors." This phrase is intentionally vague and open to interpretation, giving Congress broad discretion to determine what constitutes impeachable conduct.

The House of Representatives has the sole power to impeach federal judges. If a majority of the House votes to impeach a judge, the case is then sent to the Senate for trial. The Senate acts as a jury in the trial, with the Chief Justice of the Supreme Court presiding over the proceedings. A two-thirds majority of the Senate is required to convict a judge and remove them from office.

The Constitution for Politicians

One of the most notable instances of federal judge impeachment was the case of Samuel Chase, an Associate Justice of the Supreme Court. In 1804, the House of Representatives voted to impeach Chase for allegedly exhibiting bias and prejudice against defendants in his courtroom. Chase was ultimately acquitted by the Senate, but the case set an important precedent for the impeachment of federal judges.

In more recent times, the most high-profile case of a federal judge being impeached and removed from office was that of Alcee Hastings. Hastings was a federal judge in Florida who was impeached by the House of Representatives in 1988 on charges of perjury and conspiring to solicit a bribe. Hastings was convicted by the Senate and removed from office, becoming only the sixth federal judge in history to be removed from the bench through impeachment.

The impeachment of a federal judge is a serious matter, and it is not undertaken lightly. It is generally reserved for cases where a judge has engaged in serious misconduct or abuse of power. However, the process of impeachment is an important tool for ensuring that federal judges are held accountable for their actions and for maintaining the integrity of the judicial system.

It is worth noting that the process of impeachment is not the only way that federal judges can be removed from office. The Constitution also provides for the removal of federal judges through retirement or resignation, and Congress has the power to impeach judges for reasons other than "high crimes and misdemeanors." Additionally, federal judges are subject to disciplinary action by the Judicial Councils of their respective circuits and can be removed from cases or have their jurisdiction limited as a result of misconduct.

In conclusion, the process of impeaching federal judges is an important tool for ensuring that the judicial system remains fair and impartial. It is a serious matter that is not taken lightly and is generally reserved for cases where a judge has engaged in serious misconduct or abuse of power. Through the process of impeachment, Congress can hold federal judges accountable for their actions and maintain the integrity of the judicial system. While it is not the only means of removing a federal judge from office, it is an essential aspect of the system of checks and balances that is at the heart of American democracy.

Humorous examples of famous court cases

Humorous examples of famous court cases

The judicial system in the United States is responsible for upholding the law and ensuring justice is served. While the legal proceedings can often be serious and grave, there have been instances where court cases have taken a humorous turn. Here are some of the most notable examples of humorous court cases in American history.

Liebeck v. McDonald's Restaurants
One of the most well-known and ridiculed court cases in American history is the infamous "hot coffee" lawsuit. In 1992, Stella Liebeck sued McDonald's after she spilled a cup of their scalding-hot coffee on her lap, resulting in third-degree burns. She sued for $20,000 to cover her medical expenses, but the case quickly became a media sensation.

The case was widely mocked, with many people questioning why Liebeck was awarded such a large settlement for what they believed to be her own carelessness. However, it later came to light that McDonald's had received hundreds of complaints about their dangerously hot coffee and had ignored the issue.

United States v. Approximately 64,695 Pounds of Shark Fins
In 2012, federal authorities seized over 64,000 pounds of shark fins from a San Francisco warehouse. The fins were believed to have been illegally imported from South America, and the case became a symbol of the illegal shark fin trade.

The case itself wasn't particularly humorous, but the name of the case certainly was. The sheer absurdity of a legal case being named after a massive quantity of shark fins drew chuckles from legal experts and the public alike.

Haelan Laboratories, Inc. v. Topps Chewing Gum, Inc.
In 1947, Haelan Laboratories sued Topps Chewing Gum for including their soybean extract in their gum without permission. Topps argued that the extract was a harmless flavoring agent, but Haelan maintained that the extract was their proprietary formula and was being used without permission.

The case itself was relatively unremarkable, but it was the way in which Haelan Laboratories presented their argument that drew attention. They argued that Topps was "chewing" up their profits, and that the use of their extract was "soy un-American." The judge ultimately ruled in Haelan's favor, and the case became a lesson in how not to present a legal argument.

United States v. Article Consisting of 50,000 Cardboard Boxes, More or Less, Each Containing One Pair of Clacker Balls
In 1976, the Consumer Product Safety Commission banned the sale of clacker balls due to safety concerns. Clacker balls were made up of two hard plastic balls attached to a string, and they were prone to breaking and causing injury.

One company, Bogg's Manufacturing, refused to stop selling the clacker balls and was subsequently sued by the government. The case was named United States v. Article Consisting of 50,000 Cardboard Boxes, More or Less, Each Containing One Pair of Clacker Balls, which drew laughs from legal experts and the public alike.

Lively v. Domino's Pizza, LLC
In 2012, a man named Kenneth Lively filed a lawsuit against Domino's Pizza after he was injured while trying to climb over a fence to get to a store that had closed early. Lively argued that Domino's was responsible for his injuries because they had promised 24-hour delivery, and he had been attempting to get to a different Domino's location that was still open.

The case was ultimately dismissed, but not before it became a punchline for comedians and legal experts alike. Lively's argument

The Constitution for Politicians

that Domino's was responsible for his injuries because of their delivery promise drew widespread ridicule.

In conclusion, humor has found its way into many famous court cases throughout history. From bizarre legal arguments to humorous legal language, these cases provide a glimpse into the quirky and often unpredictable world of the law. While some of these cases may seem absurd, they are a reminder that the law is an ever-evolving and sometimes strange entity.

Despite the often-serious nature of the law, humor can play a valuable role in the legal system. Humorous court cases and legal language can help to make the law more accessible to the public, and can provide a light-hearted break from the more serious aspects of the legal system. They can also serve as cautionary tales, reminding us of the importance of sound legal reasoning and careful consideration of the facts.

While humorous court cases may be entertaining, they also serve as a reminder of the power of the law to affect people's lives in profound ways. From high-stakes legal battles to frivolous lawsuits, the law has the ability to shape society and impact individuals in significant ways. It is important to remember that while humor can provide a brief moment of levity, the law itself is a serious and often complex system that demands our attention and respect.

In the end, the legal system will always have its quirks and oddities, and we will likely continue to see humorous court cases for years to come. Whether we find these cases amusing or ridiculous, they remind us that the law is a dynamic and ever-changing entity that reflects the society in which it operates. As we continue to navigate the complex legal landscape, it is important to approach the law with a sense of humor, but also with a deep respect for its power and importance in our lives.

In conclusion, Chapter 4 of the United States Constitution plays a critical role in establishing and defining the powers of the federal judiciary. The creation of the Supreme Court and other federal courts, the appointment and qualifications of federal judges, the jurisdiction and powers of the federal courts, and the interpretation of the Constitution and federal laws are all essential to ensuring that justice is served and that the rights of individuals are protected. The judiciary is a crucial branch of government that helps maintain the balance of power and upholds the principles of democracy in the United States.

CHAPTER 5: ARTICLE IV - THE STATES

- ❖ Article IV- The States
- ❖ The Break Down
- ❖ The importance of state sovereignty
- ❖ Relationships between states and the federal government
- ❖ Obligations and responsibilities of states to each other
- ❖ Procedures for admitting new states to the Union
- ❖ Federal protection of states from invasion and domestic violence
- ❖ Funny state-specific laws and traditions

Article IV- The States

Article IV of the United States Constitution outlines the relationship between the individual states and the federal government. It establishes the duties that each state owes to the others, and to the federal government, as well as the rights and privileges that each state is entitled to under the Constitution.

The article is divided into four sections. The first section, known as the Full Faith and Credit Clause, requires each state to honor the public acts, records, and judicial proceedings of every other state. This means that a legal decision made in one state must be recognized and respected by all other states.

The second section of Article IV, known as the Privileges and Immunities Clause, requires that citizens of each state be treated equally and fairly in all other states. This means that states cannot discriminate against citizens of other states in areas such as taxation, access to courts, and property ownership.

The third section of Article IV outlines the process for admitting new states into the Union. This process involves the submission of a formal application to Congress, which must then pass a law admitting the new state.

The final section of Article IV is known as the Guarantee Clause. This section requires the federal government to protect each state from invasion and domestic violence, and to ensure that each state is governed by a republican form of government.

In summary, Article IV of the United States Constitution is a crucial component of the country's federal system. It ensures that the states are united in their commitment to uphold the Constitution and to respect one another's rights and obligations. It also sets out the procedures for expanding the Union and guarantees the safety and security of each state.

The Break Down

Harvard Law School's understanding of Article IV of the United States Constitution emphasizes the relationships between the states and the federal government, as well as the relationships between the states themselves. The article establishes the concept of "full faith and credit," which requires states to recognize the public acts, records, and judicial proceedings of other states. It also outlines the process by which new states can be admitted to the Union and provides for federal control over federal lands and territories.

Additionally, Article IV includes provisions relating to the obligations of states to each other, such as the requirement that states extradite criminals who have fled from justice in another state. The article also prohibits states from discriminating against citizens of other states and guarantees that all citizens are entitled to the privileges and immunities of citizenship in any state.

Overall, Harvard Law School's interpretation of Article IV highlights the important role of the federal government in promoting cooperation and unity among the states, while also protecting the rights of individual citizens.

Article IV of the Constitution outlines the relationships between the states and the federal government, as well as the relationships between the states themselves. Here is a breakdown of how it works:

Full Faith and Credit Clause: This clause requires that each state recognize the laws and judicial proceedings of every other state. For example, if someone gets married in one state, every other state must recognize that marriage as legally valid.

Privileges and Immunities Clause: This clause prohibits states from discriminating against citizens of other states. It ensures that citizens have the same rights and privileges, such as the right to travel or the right to own property, regardless of which state they live in.

Extradition: This refers to the process by which one state can request the return of a criminal who has fled to another state. The Constitution requires that states extradite fugitives who have committed crimes in another state.

New States and Territories: Article IV also provides a framework for admitting new states to the Union. It gives Congress the power to admit new states, and sets out the process for doing so. It also provides rules for governing territories that have not yet become states.

Republican Form of Government: Finally, Article IV guarantees that every state in the Union will have a republican form of government. This means that the people will elect their leaders and have a say in how the government is run.

Overall, Article IV is an important part of the Constitution because it ensures that the states work together and that all citizens are treated fairly, regardless of where they live. It also allows for the growth of the United States through the admission of new states, and ensures that all states operate under a similar system of government.

For Students

Article IV of the Constitution talks about how the different states in America have to work together and follow the same rules. It also says that if someone commits a crime in one state and runs away to another state, they have to be sent back to the state where they committed the crime to face punishment.

It also says that if you get married or have a driver's license in one state, those things are valid in all the other states too. This is really helpful because it means you don't have to get married or get a new driver's license every time you move to a different state!

Overall, Article IV is all about making sure that the states work together and treat each other fairly.

The importance of state sovereignty

The concept of state sovereignty is a fundamental principle in the United States Constitution, as outlined in Article IV. The principle holds that each state has independent authority over its own affairs, separate from the federal government. This concept was central to the founding of the United States and continues to play an important role in modern American politics.

State sovereignty allows individual states to govern themselves according to their own laws and customs, without undue interference from the federal government. This means that states have the power to make their own decisions on issues such as education, healthcare, taxation, and law enforcement. In many ways, state sovereignty is a key component of American democracy, as it allows citizens to have a greater say in the laws and policies that affect their daily lives.

One of the key benefits of state sovereignty is that it allows for greater experimentation and innovation in public policy. Since each state has its own unique set of challenges and circumstances, state governments are better equipped to address these issues than the federal government. For example, a state with a large rural population may have different healthcare needs than a state with a more urban population, and state sovereignty allows each state to tailor its healthcare policies accordingly.

In addition to allowing for greater experimentation and innovation, state sovereignty also helps to promote political diversity and decentralization. By allowing individual states to govern themselves according to their own laws and customs, the United States is able to avoid the pitfalls of a one-size-fits-all approach to governance. This diversity of political thought and approach helps to promote political stability and provides citizens with greater choice in the political process.

However, state sovereignty is not without its challenges. One of the key challenges is the potential for conflict between state and federal law. Since the federal government has ultimate authority over certain issues, such as immigration and interstate commerce, there is the potential for conflict when state laws conflict with federal law. In these cases, the federal government has the power to override state law, which can lead to tension and even legal battles between the states and the federal government.

Another challenge of state sovereignty is that it can sometimes lead to a lack of consistency and coordination between different states. Since each state has its own set of laws and regulations, it can be difficult to ensure consistency across state lines. This can be especially problematic in areas such as healthcare, where patients may receive different levels of care depending on which state they are in.

Despite these challenges, the principle of state sovereignty remains a vital component of American democracy. By allowing individual states to govern themselves according to their own laws and customs, the United States is able to promote greater experimentation, innovation, and diversity in public policy. This, in turn, helps to promote political stability and provides citizens with greater choice in the political process.

In conclusion, state sovereignty is a fundamental principle of the United States Constitution, as outlined in Article IV. State sovereignty allows individual states to govern themselves according to their own laws and customs, which helps to promote greater experimentation, innovation, and diversity in public policy. While there are challenges associated with state sovereignty, such as potential conflict between state and federal law, it remains a vital component of American democracy and helps to promote political stability and choice for citizens.

Relationships between states and the federal government

The relationship between states and the federal government is one of the most important and complex issues in the United States political system. Article IV of the Constitution outlines the basic relationship between states and the federal government, but many details have been worked out through legal battles and historical developments. This chapter will explore the relationships between states and the federal government, including their respective powers and the ways they interact with each other.

The Constitution defines a balance of power between the federal government and the states, known as federalism. Under this system, the federal government has specific, enumerated powers while states retain their own powers and sovereignty. This balance is reflected in the Tenth Amendment, which states that all powers not delegated to the federal government are reserved for the states.

The Constitution for Politicians

One of the most important ways that states and the federal government interact is through grants-in-aid, which are federal funds that are provided to states for specific purposes. These grants can take many forms, such as block grants or categorical grants, and can be used for a wide range of purposes including education, healthcare, and infrastructure. While these grants can provide important funding for states, they can also come with strings attached, such as specific requirements for how the funds must be used.

Another important area of interaction between states and the federal government is in the realm of taxation. The federal government has the power to levy taxes on individuals and corporations, while states also have the power to levy their own taxes. This can create complex interactions between state and federal tax codes, and can lead to conflicts over who has the power to tax certain activities or entities.

In addition to grants and taxes, states and the federal government also interact through the legal system. The federal court system has the power to hear cases that involve federal law, while state courts have jurisdiction over cases that involve state law. This can lead to conflicts between state and federal courts, as well as challenges to the supremacy of federal law over state law.

One of the most significant areas of conflict between states and the federal government is in the realm of regulation. The federal government has the power to regulate a wide range of activities, from interstate commerce to environmental protection. States also have the power to regulate certain activities within their borders, but these regulations must be in compliance with federal law. This can create tension between states and the federal government when states seek to regulate activities that the federal government sees as falling under its jurisdiction.

In recent years, some states have also sought to assert their sovereignty in areas such as immigration and gun control. These efforts have led to legal battles with the federal government, as states seek to exercise their own power in areas that have traditionally been regulated by the federal government.

Overall, the relationship between states and the federal government is a complex and constantly evolving one. While the Constitution provides a framework for this relationship, many details have been worked out through legal battles and historical developments. As states continue to assert their sovereignty and the federal government seeks to regulate more areas of activity, this relationship is likely to remain an important and contentious issue in American politics.

In conclusion, the relationship between states and the federal government is a critical component of the American political system. The balance of power between the two levels of government is reflected in the Constitution and has been worked out through legal battles and historical developments. While grants-in-aid, taxation, and the legal system are all important areas of interaction between states and the federal government, conflicts can arise when it comes to regulation and the exercise of sovereignty. As the political landscape continues to shift, it will be important for policymakers and citizens alike to understand the dynamics of this relationship and the ways in which it affects our daily lives.

Obligations and responsibilities of states to each other

Article IV of the United States Constitution sets out the obligations and responsibilities that states have to each other. These obligations are essential to maintaining a functioning and cohesive union of states and are crucial for the protection and promotion of individual rights and liberties.

One of the primary obligations of states to each other is the recognition of each other's laws, records, and judicial proceedings. This obligation is known as the Full Faith and Credit Clause, and it ensures that legal decisions made in one state are recognized and enforced in other states. For example, a driver's license issued in one state is valid in all other states due to this clause.

The Constitution for Politicians

Another important obligation of states to each other is the requirement to extradite individuals who have fled from one state to another to avoid prosecution or punishment for a crime. This obligation is known as the Extradition Clause and is essential for the proper functioning of the criminal justice system.

States are also required to treat citizens of other states equally to their own citizens. This obligation is known as the Privileges and Immunities Clause and ensures that citizens of one state are not discriminated against when traveling, conducting business, or residing in another state. For example, a citizen of New York should be able to travel to and work in California without facing discriminatory restrictions or penalties.

Additionally, states have a responsibility to cooperate with each other on a range of issues, including law enforcement, environmental protection, and public health. The Constitution grants Congress the power to regulate interstate commerce, which includes a broad range of economic and social activities that affect multiple states. As such, states are required to coordinate and collaborate with each other on a range of issues that impact interstate commerce, including transportation, trade, and labor.

Another important responsibility of states is to participate in the process of amending the Constitution. This requires the agreement of at least three-quarters of the states, which is essential for ensuring that any changes to the Constitution reflect the will of the people and the needs of the nation as a whole.

States also have a responsibility to ensure that their laws and policies do not infringe upon the rights of citizens in other states. For example, a state cannot pass a law that restricts the freedom of speech or religion of citizens from other states. This obligation is essential for protecting individual rights and ensuring that the federal system operates smoothly.

Finally, states have a responsibility to protect and promote the interests of their citizens while also respecting the rights and interests of citizens from other states. This requires states to balance their own interests with the interests of the nation as a whole, and to work collaboratively with other states to address common problems and challenges.

In recent years, the obligations and responsibilities of states to each other have been tested by a range of issues, including immigration, environmental regulation, and healthcare. These challenges have highlighted the importance of maintaining a cohesive and cooperative federal system that respects the autonomy and sovereignty of individual states while also promoting the common good.

The obligation to recognize and enforce legal decisions made in other states, for example, has been tested by the issue of same-sex marriage. Following the Supreme Court's decision in Obergefell v. Hodges in 2015, which legalized same-sex marriage across the United States, some states sought to restrict the rights of same-sex couples by refusing to recognize their marriages. However, these efforts were ultimately unsuccessful due to the Full Faith and Credit Clause, which required states to recognize and enforce legal decisions made in other states.

Similarly, the obligation to cooperate on issues of public health has been tested by the COVID-19 pandemic. While the federal government has played a significant role in coordinating the national response to the pandemic, states have also been required to work collaboratively to contain the spread of the virus and ensure the safety of their citizens.

In addition to their obligations to cooperate with each other, states also have certain responsibilities towards each other. One of the most important of these is the obligation to give "full faith and credit" to the public acts, records, and judicial proceedings of other states. This means that a legal judgment or contract made in one state must be recognized and enforced by all other states. For example, if a person gets a divorce in one state, that divorce is recognized as valid in all other states. This principle is essential for maintaining a functioning legal system across state lines and for ensuring consistency in the application of law.

States also have the responsibility to extradite individuals who are accused of committing a crime in another state. This means that if a person commits a crime in one state and then flees to another state, the second state must cooperate in the arrest and return of that individual to the state where the crime was committed. This is an important aspect of maintaining law and order across state lines and ensuring that criminals are held accountable for their actions.

Another important responsibility of states towards each other is the obligation to respect and protect the rights of citizens from other states. This includes protecting the right to travel and conduct business across state lines without discrimination or undue burden. It also includes ensuring that citizens from other states have access to basic services such as healthcare, education, and emergency services when they are within the borders of the state.

Finally, states have a responsibility to work together to address common problems and challenges. This includes issues such as environmental protection, disaster response, and transportation infrastructure. By working together, states can leverage their resources and expertise to achieve more effective solutions than they would be able to on their own.

In conclusion, the relationships between states in the United States are governed by a complex set of obligations and responsibilities. While each state retains a certain degree of autonomy and sovereignty, they are also required to cooperate with each other on a variety of issues and to respect each other's public acts and judicial proceedings. By fulfilling these obligations and responsibilities, states can work together to address common problems and challenges, promote the well-being of their citizens, and maintain the integrity of the United States as a nation.

Procedures for admitting new states to the Union

The Constitution for Politicians

The United States of America has a long and storied history of expansion, both through territorial acquisitions and the admission of new states to the Union. The process of admitting a new state is outlined in Article IV, Section 3 of the U.S. Constitution, which grants Congress the power to admit new states into the Union. However, this power is not absolute, and there are several procedures and requirements that must be met before a new state can be admitted.

The first step in the process of admitting a new state is for the territory seeking statehood to draft a constitution and apply for admission to Congress. Once this application is received, Congress will review the proposed constitution and determine if it meets the necessary requirements for statehood. One of the most important requirements is that the proposed state constitution must be republican in form, meaning that it must provide for a representative form of government in which the power ultimately rests with the people.

If Congress determines that the proposed constitution meets the requirements for statehood, it will pass an act of admission, which is essentially a law that formally admits the territory as a new state. The act of admission will specify the new state's boundaries, establish its government structure, and set the conditions under which it will be admitted to the Union. Once the act of admission is signed into law by the President, the new state is officially admitted to the Union and granted all the rights and privileges of statehood.

While the process of admitting new states to the Union is well-established, it is not without controversy. One of the most contentious issues related to statehood is the question of whether a new state should be admitted as a slave or free state. This issue was at the heart of the debate over the admission of Missouri in the early 19th century, which ultimately resulted in the Missouri Compromise of 1820. Under this compromise, Missouri was admitted as a slave state, while Maine was admitted as a free state, and a line was drawn at the 36° 30' parallel to designate which territories could allow slavery and which could not.

Another important issue related to the admission of new states is the question of whether the new state will have equal representation in the Senate. This issue was particularly contentious during the early years of the Republic, when there were concerns about maintaining a balance of power between the northern and southern states. The solution was the "equal footing" principle, which holds that all states admitted to the Union must have equal rights and privileges as the original 13 states.

The process for admitting new states to the Union has been used many times throughout American history. From the admission of Vermont in 1791 to the most recent admission of Hawaii in 1959, the United States has grown and expanded over the centuries, adding new states with unique cultures, histories, and perspectives. However, the process of admitting new states is not always straightforward, and it can take many years of debate and negotiation before a new state is officially admitted.

One recent example of the difficulties involved in admitting a new state is the case of Puerto Rico. Puerto Rico has been a U.S. territory since 1898, and its residents are U.S. citizens. However, Puerto Rico does not have voting representation in Congress, and its status as a territory has long been a subject of debate. In recent years, there have been calls for Puerto Rico to be admitted as the 51st state, but the issue remains unresolved.

In conclusion, the process of admitting new states to the Union is an important part of American history and government. While the process is well-established, it is not without controversy, and the admission of new states can have significant implications for the balance of power in Congress and the country as a whole. Despite these challenges, the procedures for admitting new states to the Union have generally been successful in maintaining a balance between the power of the federal government and the rights and interests of individual states.

The admission of new states is a complex and often contentious process, but it is an important part of American democracy. By providing a means for new communities to join the Union, the process ensures that the United States remains a dynamic and evolving nation. As the country continues to grow and change, the procedures for admitting new states will undoubtedly be tested and refined, but the fundamental principles of statehood and democracy that underlie these procedures will remain strong.

Federal protection of states from invasion and domestic violence

The Constitution of the United States sets out the principles that govern the country's federal system, defining the powers of the federal government and the states. One of the critical roles of the federal government is to protect the states from invasion and domestic violence. This protection is a critical aspect of the country's security and is an essential responsibility of the federal government.

The framers of the Constitution were keenly aware of the dangers posed by foreign invasion and domestic violence. They recognized that the states, acting alone, might not be able to protect themselves adequately against such threats. Therefore, they included provisions in the Constitution that authorized the federal government to provide protection to the states.

Article IV, Section 4 of the Constitution provides that "The United States shall guarantee to every State in this Union a Republican Form of Government, and shall protect each of them against Invasion; and on Application of the Legislature, or of the Executive (when the Legislature cannot be convened), against domestic Violence." This clause, known as the Guarantee Clause, sets out the federal government's responsibility to ensure that each state has a republican form of government and to protect the states against invasion and domestic violence.

The federal government's power to protect the states is derived from the Constitution's Supremacy Clause, which provides that federal law is the supreme law of the land. This means that federal law supersedes state law, and the federal government has the authority to enforce federal law to protect the states from threats to their security.

The Constitution for Politicians

The federal government has several mechanisms for protecting the states from invasion and domestic violence. One of the most significant of these is the military. The Constitution grants Congress the power to raise and support armies, and the President is the Commander-in-Chief of the armed forces. The military can be used to protect the states from external threats, such as invasion, and to assist in the event of domestic violence.

The federal government can also provide financial assistance to the states to help them meet their security needs. The Department of Homeland Security, for example, works with state and local authorities to coordinate efforts to prevent and respond to threats of terrorism and other forms of domestic violence. Additionally, the federal government can provide grants and other forms of funding to the states to help them improve their emergency response capabilities.

In addition to these measures, the federal government can also use the courts to protect the states from invasion and domestic violence. The Constitution grants the federal courts the power to hear cases and controversies arising under federal law, including cases involving threats to the states' security. The federal government can use the courts to seek injunctions and other remedies to prevent or address threats to the states.

The federal government's responsibility to protect the states from invasion and domestic violence has been tested throughout American history. During the Civil War, for example, the federal government used its military and judicial powers to protect the states from secession and rebellion. In the 20th century, the federal government played a critical role in protecting the states from threats such as the Japanese attack on Pearl Harbor and the terrorist attacks of September 11, 2001.

The federal government's responsibility to protect the states is not absolute, however. The Guarantee Clause does not provide a detailed roadmap for how the federal government should fulfill its responsibility to protect the states, and there is often debate over the appropriate scope and nature of federal intervention. Some argue that the federal government's role should be limited to providing financial and logistical support to the states, while others argue that the federal government should take a more active role in protecting the states.

In conclusion, the federal government's responsibility to protect the states from invasion and domestic violence is a critical aspect of American government and history. The Constitution's Guarantee Clause provides the framework for federal protection of the states, and the federal government has several mechanisms for fulfilling this responsibility, including the military, the National Guard, and other law enforcement agencies. The importance of this responsibility was demonstrated during events such as the Whiskey Rebellion, the Civil War, and the civil rights movement.

As the country continues to face new challenges, such as cyberattacks and other emerging threats, the federal government's role in protecting the states from invasion and domestic violence will remain crucial. It is essential that federal and state governments work together to ensure the safety and security of all citizens, while also upholding the principles of democracy and the rule of law. By maintaining a strong and effective system of federal protection, the United States can continue to thrive as a beacon of freedom and opportunity for all.

Funny state-specific laws and traditions

The United States is known for having some unusual and amusing laws, many of which are state-specific. From wacky traditions to bizarre regulations, each state has its own unique set of rules and customs that can leave outsiders scratching their heads in confusion. In this chapter, we will explore some of the funniest state-specific laws and traditions across the country.

Let's start with Alabama, where it is illegal to wear a fake mustache in church that causes laughter. It's unclear what led to this law being passed, but one can only imagine the shenanigans that must have taken place in Alabama churches before it was enacted. Another amusing Alabama law requires that you keep your car headlights on if you are driving in the daytime and can't see because of smoke, fog, or rain.

Moving on to Alaska, the state has a tradition called the "Frozen Dead Guy Days." The festival, held annually in the town of Nederland, Colorado, celebrates the life of a Norwegian man who died and was cryogenically frozen in a shed in the town in the 1990s. The event includes coffin races, frozen turkey bowling, and a parade featuring a "Grandpa Bredo" lookalike.

In Arizona, it is illegal for donkeys to sleep in bathtubs. This law was passed after a man left his donkey in his bathtub overnight, and it fell asleep and could not be removed. The man was forced to call the fire department to remove the donkey, leading to the creation of this unique law.

In California, it is illegal to whistle for a lost canary before 7 am. This law is likely intended to prevent disturbing neighbors with early-morning noise, but it's hard to imagine a scenario where someone would need to whistle for a lost canary at such an early hour.

Moving on to Colorado, the state has a law that prohibits the use of dildos. This law, which was struck down by a federal court in 2007, prohibited the sale or use of sex toys, leading to widespread criticism and ridicule.

In Connecticut, it is illegal to cross a street while walking on your hands. While this law is unlikely to be enforced, it's hard to imagine why someone would want to cross a street on their hands in the first place.

In Delaware, it is illegal to sell dog hair. This law was enacted in response to a scam in which dog hair was sold as "Angora wool." It's unclear if anyone has been prosecuted under this law, but it remains on the books to this day.

The Constitution for Politicians

In Florida, it is illegal to tie an elephant to a parking meter or street lamp. This law is likely intended to prevent people from using elephants as a means of transportation or as a form of entertainment.

Moving on to Georgia, it is illegal to tie a giraffe to a telephone pole or street lamp. This law is likely a similar preventative measure to the Florida law against tying elephants to public fixtures.

In Hawaii, it is illegal to place a coin in your ear. While this law is unlikely to be enforced, it's interesting to consider why it was enacted in the first place.

In Idaho, it is illegal for a man to give his sweetheart a box of candy weighing less than fifty pounds. This law, which dates back to the early 1900s, was intended to ensure that women were properly courted by their suitors.

In Illinois, it is illegal to fall asleep in a cheese factory. While this law may seem random, it was likely passed as a safety measure to prevent workers from falling asleep on the job and endangering themselves or others.

In Indiana, it is illegal to catch a fish with your bare hands. This law is likely intended to promote safe fishing practices and prevent injuries.

In Iowa, it is illegal for a man with a mustache to kiss a woman in public. This law may have been intended to prevent public displays of affection, but it is now widely regarded as outdated and ridiculous.

In Kansas, it is illegal to serve wine in teacups. This law is thought to have originated during Prohibition, when some people would try to disguise alcohol as tea in order to avoid detection by authorities.

In Kentucky, it is illegal to dye a duckling blue and offer it for sale unless more than six are for sale at once. This law is intended to protect the welfare of animals by preventing them from being sold in small quantities, which can lead to loneliness and neglect.

The Constitution for Politicians

In Louisiana, it is illegal to send a surprise pizza delivery to someone's home without their consent. This law is intended to prevent unwanted and potentially dangerous deliveries, and is sometimes referred to as the "pizza stalking" law.

These state-specific laws and traditions may seem strange or humorous, but they reflect the unique history and culture of each state. They also serve as a reminder that laws are not always rational or logical, and that there is often a complex interplay between social norms, legal precedent, and political power.

While some of these laws may seem frivolous or outdated, they can still have a real impact on people's lives. For example, the law in Indiana against catching fish with bare hands may seem like a joke, but it can actually result in fines or even criminal charges for those who violate it. Similarly, the law in Iowa about mustached men kissing women in public may seem silly, but it can reinforce harmful gender stereotypes and perpetuate discrimination.

Despite their quirks and peculiarities, state-specific laws and traditions are an important part of American culture and history. They serve as a reminder that laws are not fixed or unchanging, but are instead constantly evolving and adapting to the needs and values of society. As such, they offer a fascinating window into the past, present, and future of American law and society.

CHAPTER 6: ARTICLE V - THE AMENDMENT PROCESS

❖ Article V - The Amendment Process
❖ The Break Down
❖ Procedures for amending the Constitution
❖ The difficulty of amending the Constitution
❖ Proposal and ratification of amendments
❖ Limits on the powers of amendments
❖ Humorous examples of proposed amendments

Chapter 6 explores the amendment process of the United States Constitution. The amendment process is a crucial aspect of the Constitution, as it allows for the document to evolve and change to meet the needs of the country over time. However, the amendment process is not without its challenges, including the difficulty of amending the Constitution and the limits on the powers of amendments. This chapter will delve into these issues, as well as humorous examples of proposed amendments.

Article V - The Amendment Process

Article V of the United States Constitution outlines the process for amending the Constitution. It states that the Constitution may be amended by a two-thirds vote of both the House of Representatives and the Senate, followed by ratification by three-fourths of the states.

Alternatively, a constitutional convention may be called by two-thirds of the state legislatures, which can then propose amendments that must be ratified by three-fourths of the states.

This process for amending the Constitution is deliberately difficult, as the framers wanted to ensure that any changes to the Constitution were made thoughtfully and with broad support. Since the Constitution was written in 1787, it has been amended 27 times, with the most recent amendment (the 27th Amendment) being ratified in 1992.

The Break Down

Harvard Law School explains that Article V of the United States Constitution outlines the process for amending the Constitution. The amendment process requires a two-step process, which involves the proposal of the amendment and the subsequent ratification of the amendment.

The first step of the amendment process involves the proposal of the amendment. There are two methods for proposing amendments:

By Congress: The first method is for Congress to propose an amendment with a two-thirds vote in both the House of Representatives and the Senate. Once the amendment is proposed, it is sent to the states for ratification.

By convention: The second method is for a convention called for by two-thirds of the states to propose an amendment. This method has never been used in the history of the United States.

The second step of the amendment process involves the ratification of the amendment. Once an amendment is proposed, it must be ratified by three-fourths of the states in order to become part of the Constitution. There are two methods for ratifying amendments:

By state legislatures: The first method is for the amendment to be ratified by three-fourths of the state legislatures.

The Constitution for Politicians

By conventions: The second method is for the amendment to be ratified by three-fourths of the states through conventions. This method has only been used once, for the ratification of the 21st Amendment.

Once an amendment is ratified, it becomes part of the Constitution and has the same legal standing as any other part of the Constitution.

It is important to note that the amendment process is intentionally difficult in order to ensure that changes to the Constitution are made only when there is broad consensus and support for the change. Since the Constitution was ratified in 1788, there have been only 27 amendments, with the most recent being added in 1992.

For Students

Article V of the United States Constitution is like a rulebook for how to change the rules of the game. It explains that if the people in charge of the country (the government) want to make a big change to the rules (like adding a new rule or taking away an old one), they have to follow a specific process.

First, they have to come up with a proposal for the change. This could be done by the government or by regular people who want to suggest a change.

Next, the proposal has to be approved by either two-thirds of the Congress (the group of people who make the laws) or two-thirds of the states.

Then, the proposal has to be sent out to all the states so they can decide whether they want to approve it. If three-fourths of the states approve the proposal, it becomes a new rule that everyone has to follow.

This process is designed to make sure that big changes to the rules are only made if a lot of people agree that it's a good idea.

Procedures for amending the Constitution

The Constitution of the United States is the supreme law of the land, providing the framework for the government of the country. It is a living document that can be amended, or changed, as the needs of the country and its people evolve over time. However, the process for amending the Constitution is deliberately difficult and time-consuming to ensure that amendments are not made impulsively or without due consideration.

Article V of the Constitution outlines the procedures for amending the document. The amendment process can be initiated by either Congress or the states, and it involves several steps that must be completed before an amendment can be added to the Constitution.

The first step in the amendment process is the proposal of an amendment. This can be done in one of two ways. The first way is for Congress to propose an amendment by a two-thirds vote of both the House of Representatives and the Senate. Once an amendment has been proposed, it is sent to the states for consideration. The second way to propose an amendment is for the states to call for a constitutional convention. This has never been done in the history of the United States, but if it were to occur, the convention would propose amendments that would then be sent to the states for consideration.

Once an amendment has been proposed, it must be ratified before it can be added to the Constitution. There are two ways that an amendment can be ratified. The first way is for three-fourths of the states to approve the amendment. This is done through a process known as state ratifying conventions, in which special elections are held to determine whether the states approve of the amendment. The second way to ratify an amendment is for three-fourths of the state legislatures to approve it.

The Constitution for Politicians

The amendment process is deliberately difficult and time-consuming to ensure that amendments are not made impulsively or without due consideration. This process has been used to add 27 amendments to the Constitution since it was ratified in 1788. Some of the most significant amendments include the Bill of Rights, which includes the first ten amendments to the Constitution and guarantees many of the individual freedoms that Americans enjoy today.

One of the most controversial amendments to the Constitution was the 18th Amendment, which prohibited the manufacture, sale, and transportation of alcoholic beverages in the United States. This amendment was ratified in 1919 but was later repealed by the 21st Amendment in 1933, showing that the amendment process can be used to correct mistakes made in the past.

Another significant amendment is the 19th Amendment, which granted women the right to vote. This amendment was ratified in 1920, after a long and difficult struggle by suffragettes and other advocates for women's rights. The 19th Amendment was a major step forward for women's equality in the United States.

The amendment process has also been used to address issues related to civil rights and equality. The 13th Amendment abolished slavery in the United States, while the 14th Amendment granted citizenship to all persons born or naturalized in the United States, including former slaves. The 15th Amendment granted African American men the right to vote. Later, the 24th Amendment prohibited poll taxes, which had been used to prevent many African Americans from voting. Finally, the 26th Amendment lowered the voting age to 18, giving young people a voice in the democratic process.

In conclusion, the amendment process is an important part of the Constitution of the United States. It allows the document to evolve and change as the needs of the country and its people change over time. The amendment process is deliberately difficult and time-consuming to ensure that amendments are not made impulsively or without due consideration. While the process has been used to address a wide range of issues, from civil rights to the regulation of alcohol, it remains an important safeguard against hasty and ill-considered changes to the Constitution.

It is important to note that while the amendment process provides a means of changing the Constitution, it is not the only way in which the document can be interpreted and applied. Over the years, the Supreme Court has played a critical role in interpreting the Constitution and shaping American law through its decisions.

Nevertheless, the amendment process remains an important aspect of American democracy and government. It allows for changes to be made to the Constitution that reflect the will of the people and the evolving needs of the country. As the United States continues to face new challenges and opportunities in the years to come, the amendment process will likely continue to play an important role in shaping the future of the country.

The difficulty of amending the Constitution

The Constitution of the United States is a foundational document that sets forth the framework of the American government and the rights and freedoms of its citizens. It has been amended only 27 times since its ratification in 1788, a reflection of the significant effort required to change its provisions. The amendment process is deliberately difficult, requiring broad consensus among different branches of government and the American people. This chapter explores the reasons why amending the Constitution is so difficult, the historical attempts to amend the Constitution, and the contemporary debates surrounding proposed amendments.

One of the primary reasons why amending the Constitution is so difficult is that it requires broad consensus among different branches of government and the American people. The Constitution sets forth a complex process for amending its provisions, which requires the support of two-thirds of both the House of Representatives and the Senate, as well as the ratification of three-fourths of the states. This means that any proposed amendment must be able to garner broad support among members of Congress, state legislatures, and the American public.

Additionally, the process of amending the Constitution is time-consuming and arduous. The amendment process can take years, if not decades, to complete, requiring extensive lobbying and public education campaigns to build support for the proposed amendment. In many cases, proposed amendments have failed to gain traction because of a lack of public support or opposition from powerful interest groups.

Historically, there have been many attempts to amend the Constitution that have failed. Some of the most notable examples include the Equal Rights Amendment (ERA) and the Balanced Budget Amendment. The ERA was first proposed in 1923 and sought to guarantee equal rights for women in all aspects of American life. Despite being ratified by 35 states, the ERA failed to meet the required threshold of 38 states by the deadline for ratification in 1982, and it has not been ratified since.

Similarly, the Balanced Budget Amendment, which would require the federal government to balance its budget each year, has been proposed several times since the 1930s but has never been ratified. Supporters argue that such an amendment is necessary to prevent the federal government from accruing unsustainable levels of debt, while opponents argue that it would be impractical and could lead to harmful cuts in social programs.

In recent years, there have been several proposed amendments that have generated significant debate and discussion. One example is the proposal to overturn the Supreme Court's Citizens United decision, which held that corporations have the same free speech rights as individuals and opened the door to unlimited political spending by corporations and other groups. Proponents argue that the amendment is necessary to curb the influence of wealthy special interests in American politics, while opponents argue that it would infringe on free speech rights and could have unintended consequences.

Another proposed amendment that has generated significant discussion is the proposal to abolish the Electoral College and elect the president by popular vote. Supporters argue that the Electoral College is an outdated system that can result in the election of a president who does not win the popular vote, as happened in the 2000 and 2016 presidential elections. Opponents argue that the Electoral College is a vital part of the American political system and helps ensure that smaller states have a voice in the presidential election.

Despite the difficulties and challenges of amending the Constitution, the amendment process remains a critical part of American democracy. It allows the Constitution to evolve and change as the needs of the country and its people change over time. The amendment process is a powerful tool for ensuring that the Constitution remains relevant and responsive to the needs of the American people, while also preserving the fundamental principles and values that have made the United States a beacon of democracy and freedom around the world.

Proposal and ratification of amendments

Proposal and ratification of amendments to the United States Constitution is a long and complex process that involves multiple steps and requires the involvement of both the federal government and the states. This process has been intentionally designed to be difficult to ensure that any changes made to the Constitution are deliberate, thoughtful, and widely supported.

The Constitution of the United States has been amended only 27 times since it was adopted in 1787. This low number of amendments is a testament to the difficulty of amending the Constitution, as well as the importance placed on the document as the cornerstone of American government and society.

The process of proposing amendments begins with Congress, which has the power to initiate the amendment process through a two-thirds vote in both the House of Representatives and the Senate. This is the most common method of proposing amendments and has been used for all 27 amendments. Once an amendment is proposed, it must be ratified by three-fourths of the states before it can become part of the Constitution.

There are two ways that amendments can be ratified: by state legislatures or by state conventions. The first method, which has been used for all but one amendment, involves the amendment being sent to the state legislatures for ratification. Once three-fourths of the state legislatures have approved the amendment, it becomes part of the Constitution.

The second method of ratification, by state conventions, has only been used once in the amendment process, for the ratification of the 21st Amendment, which repealed Prohibition. Under this method, the amendment is sent to state conventions for ratification instead of the state legislatures. The conventions are made up of elected delegates who are responsible for voting on whether to ratify the amendment. Once three-fourths of the state conventions have approved the amendment, it becomes part of the Constitution.

The process of amending the Constitution is intentionally difficult to ensure that any changes made to the document are widely supported and carefully considered. This difficulty is reflected in the fact that only 27 amendments have been ratified in over 230 years, despite the many challenges and changes faced by the United States during that time.

One of the challenges of amending the Constitution is the high threshold for approval. A proposed amendment must be approved by two-thirds of both the House of Representatives and the Senate before it can be sent to the states for ratification. This requirement ensures that any amendment has broad support from both the legislative branch and the federal government before it can move forward in the process.

Another challenge of amending the Constitution is the requirement that the amendment be ratified by three-fourths of the states. This means that a proposed amendment must be approved by at least 38 of the 50 states before it can become part of the Constitution. This high threshold for approval ensures that any amendment has broad support from the states, which are considered to be the cornerstone of American democracy.

The process of amending the Constitution is also complicated by the fact that the amendment process has become politicized in recent years. Some groups and individuals have proposed amendments to the Constitution to advance their political agendas, leading to contentious debates and opposition from those who disagree with the proposed changes.

One example of a proposed amendment that has faced opposition is the Equal Rights Amendment, which was first proposed in 1972 and sought to prohibit discrimination on the basis of sex. Despite being approved by Congress and ratified by 38 states, the amendment has not been added to the Constitution due to a variety of legal and political challenges.

The difficulty of amending the Constitution is also reflected in the fact that some issues have been addressed through alternative means, such as Supreme Court decisions or federal legislation, rather than through the amendment process. For example, the Supreme Court's decision in Brown v. Board of Education in 1954, which declared segregation in public schools to be unconstitutional, is often considered a landmark moment in the Civil Rights Movement, and it served as a catalyst for desegregation efforts throughout the country. Similarly, the passage of the Civil Rights Act of 1964 and the Voting Rights Act of 1965 were major legislative achievements that helped address issues of discrimination and voting rights, respectively.

However, these alternative means of addressing issues are not without their own limitations. Supreme Court decisions can be overturned or limited by future Court decisions, and federal legislation can be repealed or modified by Congress. In contrast, amendments to the Constitution are considered to be the most permanent and difficult to alter means of addressing issues.

The Constitution for Politicians

The proposal and ratification of amendments to the Constitution is a deliberate and multi-step process that reflects the difficulty and importance of amending the document. To propose an amendment, there are two methods outlined in Article V of the Constitution:

Proposal by Congress: An amendment can be proposed by a two-thirds vote in both the House of Representatives and the Senate. This is the most common method of proposing amendments, with 33 of the 27 amendments to the Constitution being proposed in this way.

Proposal by Convention: An amendment can also be proposed by a convention called for by two-thirds of the state legislatures. This method has never been used to propose an amendment, but it remains a possible option.

Once an amendment has been proposed, it must be ratified by the states. There are also two methods for ratification:

Ratification by State Legislatures: An amendment can be ratified by three-fourths of the state legislatures. This is the most common method of ratification, with 26 of the 27 amendments being ratified in this way.

Ratification by Conventions: An amendment can also be ratified by conventions in three-fourths of the states. This method has only been used once, for the 21st Amendment, which repealed Prohibition.

The process for amending the Constitution is intentionally difficult and time-consuming. This is because the Constitution is meant to be a stable and enduring document, not subject to frequent changes or whims of popular opinion. The amendment process requires broad support from both Congress and the states, and it ensures that changes to the Constitution are carefully considered and thoroughly debated.

Despite its difficulty, the amendment process has been used successfully throughout American history to address important issues and expand rights and protections for citizens. The Bill of Rights, which includes the first ten amendments to the Constitution, is perhaps the most well-known example of the amendment process at work. The 13th, 14th, and 15th Amendments, which abolished slavery, granted citizenship to former slaves, and guaranteed voting rights regardless of race, respectively, are also significant examples of the amendment process being used to address major social issues.

However, there have also been proposed amendments that were not ratified by the required number of states, demonstrating the challenges of getting widespread support for a constitutional amendment. For example, the Equal Rights Amendment, which was first proposed in 1923 and sought to guarantee equal rights for women under the law, was not ratified by the required number of states before its deadline passed in 1982. Efforts to revive the ERA continue to this day.

In conclusion, the proposal and ratification of amendments to the Constitution is a challenging and multi-step process that reflects the importance of the document and the need for careful consideration of changes. While the process has been used successfully to address important issues throughout American history, it remains difficult to achieve widespread support for a constitutional amendment. The amendment process serves as a critical safeguard against hasty and ill-considered changes to the Constitution, while also providing a means for progress and expansion of rights and protections for citizens.

Limits on the powers of amendments

The power to amend the Constitution of the United States is an important tool for ensuring that the document remains relevant and responsive to the changing needs of the country. However, the Constitution also includes limits on the powers of amendments. These limits are designed to protect the fundamental principles of the Constitution and ensure that the document remains a stable and enduring foundation for American government.

One of the most significant limits on the powers of amendments is the Bill of Rights. The Bill of Rights is a set of ten amendments that were added to the Constitution in 1791. These amendments are designed to protect the fundamental rights and freedoms of American citizens, such as the freedom of speech, the right to bear arms, and the right to a fair trial. The Bill of Rights is considered to be one of the most important and enduring elements of the Constitution, and any attempt to amend it would be met with strong resistance from the American public.

Another limit on the powers of amendments is the requirement for ratification by the states. In order for an amendment to be added to the Constitution, it must be approved by a two-thirds vote in both houses of Congress or by a convention called for by two-thirds of the state legislatures. Once an amendment is proposed, it must be ratified by three-fourths of the states in order to become part of the Constitution. This requirement for ratification by the states ensures that amendments reflect the will of the people, rather than the interests of a small group of individuals.

The process for amending the Constitution is deliberately difficult and time-consuming. This is because the Founding Fathers recognized that the Constitution was an important and enduring document that should only be changed under the most serious of circumstances. In order to amend the Constitution, there must be a broad consensus among the American people that the amendment is necessary and appropriate. This consensus is reflected in the requirement for a two-thirds vote in Congress or a convention called for by two-thirds of the state legislatures.

The Constitution also includes limits on the content of amendments. For example, the Constitution prohibits amendments that would deprive states of equal representation in the Senate, or that would allow Congress to regulate or abolish slavery. These limits ensure that the fundamental principles of the Constitution, such as federalism and individual rights, are protected from arbitrary or capricious changes.

In addition to these formal limits on the powers of amendments, there are also informal limits that reflect the cultural and political norms of American society. For example, there is a strong tradition of respecting the rights and freedoms of individuals, and any amendment that threatened these rights would be met with widespread opposition.

Similarly, there is a tradition of federalism in American government, and any amendment that threatened the rights and powers of the states would be met with resistance.

Despite these limits on the powers of amendments, the Constitution has been amended 27 times since its adoption in 1787. Some of these amendments have been controversial, such as the 18th Amendment, which prohibited the sale and consumption of alcohol, and the 21st Amendment, which repealed the 18th Amendment. Other amendments, such as the 19th Amendment, which gave women the right to vote, have been celebrated as important milestones in the fight for equality and justice.

The process for amending the Constitution remains an important and essential part of American government. While the process is deliberately difficult and time-consuming, it ensures that any changes to the Constitution reflect the will of the American people and are in line with the fundamental principles of the document. As the country continues to evolve and change, the amendment process will remain a critical tool for ensuring that the Constitution remains a stable and enduring foundation for American government.

Humorous examples of proposed amendments

Over the years, there have been many proposed amendments to the United States Constitution, some serious and some not so serious. While many amendments have been proposed with good intentions, others have been proposed more as a joke or a form of political satire. Here are some humorous examples of proposed amendments:

➢ The Right to Drink Alcohol: During the era of Prohibition, which lasted from 1920 to 1933, the 18th Amendment banned the manufacture, sale, and transportation of alcohol in the United States. However, some people believed that the government had no right to interfere with their right to drink alcohol, and proposed an amendment to the Constitution to ensure that right. The proposed amendment read, "The right of citizens of the United States to consume alcoholic beverages shall not be infringed."

➢ The Right to Keep and Bear Arms...and Wear Them Too: The Second Amendment to the Constitution guarantees the right to keep and bear arms, but it doesn't say anything about wearing them. In response to this oversight, a proposed amendment in the 1990s sought to add the phrase "and wear them too" to the Second Amendment.

➢ The Right to a Good Haircut: In 1972, a man named Robert Byrne proposed an amendment to the Constitution that would guarantee every American the right to a good haircut. Byrne argued that the government should ensure that hairdressers were properly trained and licensed, and that every citizen had access to a competent barber or hairstylist.

➢ The Right to Vote for Animals: In 2012, a group called the "Dog PAC" proposed an amendment to the Constitution that would give animals the right to vote. The proposed amendment would have allowed pet owners to cast a vote on behalf of their pets, ensuring that their interests were represented in the political process.

➢ The Right to Life for Fertilized Eggs: The debate over abortion has led to several proposed amendments to the Constitution, including one that would grant legal personhood to fertilized eggs. The proposed amendment would have banned abortion and many forms of contraception, and would have created a legal basis for prosecuting women who had abortions.

While these proposed amendments may seem humorous or absurd, they serve as a reminder of the important role that the Constitution plays in American society. The Constitution is a serious document that outlines the fundamental principles of American democracy, and any proposed amendments must be carefully considered and debated. While some proposed amendments may be tongue-in-cheek or satirical, they still play a role in shaping the national conversation and reflecting the values and concerns of the American people.

conclusion

In conclusion, the amendment process is an essential component of the United States Constitution. It allows the document to evolve and change as the needs of the country change over time. However, the process is not without its challenges, including the difficulty of amending the Constitution and the limits on the powers of amendments. Despite these obstacles, the amendment process has been successfully used to address a wide range of issues throughout American history, from civil rights to the regulation of alcohol. Additionally, some proposed amendments have been more humorous than serious, serving as a reminder of the importance of careful consideration when proposing changes to the Constitution. Overall, the amendment process remains an important safeguard against hasty and ill-considered changes to the fundamental document that governs the United States.

The Constitution for Politicians

CHAPTER 7: ARTICLE VI - FEDERAL SUPREMACY

❖   Article VI - Federal Supremacy
❖   The Break Down
❖   The importance of the Constitution as the supreme law of the land
❖   How the federal government's power is balanced against the states
❖   The supremacy of the federal government over state governments
❖   The supremacy of federal law over state law
❖   Oaths of office for federal and state officials
❖   Fun examples of federal vs. state power struggles

The relationship between the federal government and state governments is a fundamental aspect of the American political system. While the Constitution establishes a system of federalism that divides powers between the federal and state governments, conflicts can arise between the two levels of government over the interpretation and exercise of those powers. This can lead to power struggles and legal battles that sometimes result in humorous or unexpected outcomes. In this chapter, we will explore some of the funniest and most interesting examples of federal versus state power struggles.

Article VI - Federal Supremacy

Article VI of the United States Constitution is commonly known as the Supremacy Clause. It establishes that the federal Constitution, federal laws enacted pursuant to it, and treaties entered into by the United States are the supreme law of the land, meaning they take precedence over state laws and constitutions. The Supremacy Clause also mandates that all state and federal officials are bound by oath or affirmation to support the Constitution. This provision ensures that the federal government has the power to enforce its laws and regulations, and that the rights and protections guaranteed by the Constitution are upheld at all levels of government.

The Break Down

According to Harvard Law School, Article VI of the United States Constitution establishes the principle of federal supremacy. This means that the Constitution, federal laws, and treaties take precedence over state laws and constitutions. In particular, the article states that "this Constitution, and the laws of the United States which shall be made in pursuance thereof; and all treaties made, or which shall be made, under the authority of the United States, shall be the supreme law of the land; and the judges in every state shall be bound thereby, anything in the constitution or laws of any state to the contrary notwithstanding."

This article is important because it ensures that there is consistency and uniformity in the application of federal law across all states. It also prevents states from enacting laws that conflict with federal law or the Constitution. In cases where there is a conflict between federal and state law, federal law takes precedence and must be followed.

Overall, Article VI reinforces the idea of a strong and unified federal government, with the power to establish and enforce laws that apply to all citizens and states within the United States.

According to the Supreme Court, the limitations to Article VI's federal supremacy clause include the requirement that federal law must be made in pursuance of the Constitution in order to be considered supreme over state law. Additionally, the Court has held that the federal government cannot commandeer state officials to enforce federal law, and that states retain certain powers and immunities from federal interference under the Tenth Amendment. Finally, the Court has also recognized the principle of dual sovereignty, which allows states to exercise their own independent authority in certain areas, even when federal law may conflict with state law.

For Students

Article VI of the Constitution says that the Constitution, the laws made under it, and the treaties made by the United States are the highest laws of the land. This means that if there is a conflict between state laws and federal laws, the federal laws win.

However, the Supreme Court has said that the federal government can only use its powers in ways that are allowed by the Constitution. This means that if the federal government tries to do something that is not allowed by the Constitution, the Supreme Court can say that it is not allowed and strike it down.

For example, if the federal government tried to make a law that said people couldn't practice their religion, the Supreme Court would say that this is not allowed by the Constitution and strike it down.

The importance of the Constitution as the supreme law of the land

The United States Constitution is the supreme law of the land. This means that no law or government action can contradict the principles and provisions laid out in the Constitution. The Constitution is the foundation of American democracy and plays a crucial role in maintaining the balance of power between the federal government and the states.

The importance of the Constitution as the supreme law of the land is reflected in several key ways. First and foremost, the Constitution provides the framework for the federal government and its relationship with the states. It outlines the powers and responsibilities of the three branches of government – the legislative, executive, and judicial – and establishes a system of checks and balances to prevent any one branch from becoming too powerful.

The Constitution for Politicians

In addition, the Constitution protects individual rights and liberties by limiting the government's ability to infringe upon them. The Bill of Rights, the first ten amendments to the Constitution, guarantees essential rights such as freedom of speech, religion, and the press, as well as the right to bear arms and the right to a fair trial.

Another key aspect of the Constitution's importance as the supreme law of the land is its ability to adapt and evolve over time. The Constitution has been amended twenty-seven times since its ratification in 1788, reflecting changes in society and addressing issues that were not anticipated by the original framers. For example, the 19th Amendment, ratified in 1920, granted women the right to vote, while the 26th Amendment, ratified in 1971, lowered the voting age from 21 to 18.

The Constitution also serves as a symbol of American democracy and a source of national pride. It embodies the values and principles that make the United States unique among nations, including the rule of law, individual rights, and equal protection under the law.

Despite its importance, the Constitution is not without its flaws and limitations. One limitation is that its interpretation can be subjective, with different individuals and groups interpreting its provisions in different ways. This has led to heated debates and disagreements over issues such as gun control, abortion, and same-sex marriage, with both sides claiming to have the Constitution on their side.

Another limitation is that the Constitution can be difficult to amend. This is intentional, as it ensures that amendments are not made impulsively or without due consideration. However, it can also make it challenging to address pressing issues that require constitutional changes, such as the role of money in politics or the balance of power between the federal government and the states.

In conclusion, the Constitution's status as the supreme law of the land is essential to the functioning of American democracy. It provides a framework for government, protects individual rights and liberties, and serves as a symbol of national identity. While it is not without its flaws and limitations, its ability to adapt and evolve over time reflects the dynamic nature of American society and its commitment to the principles of democracy and freedom.

How the federal government's power is balanced against the states

The United States Constitution established a federal system of government, in which power is shared between the federal government and the states. While the federal government has significant powers, the Constitution also includes provisions designed to balance federal power against state power. This chapter will explore the ways in which the federal government's power is balanced against the states.

One of the most significant ways in which the federal government's power is balanced against the states is through the principle of federalism. Under federalism, power is shared between the federal government and the states, with each level of government having its own set of powers and responsibilities. This system of shared power helps to prevent the federal government from becoming too powerful, while also ensuring that states have a significant role in governing themselves.

Another way in which the federal government's power is balanced against the states is through the principle of separation of powers. The Constitution divides the federal government into three branches – the legislative, executive, and judicial branches – with each branch having its own set of powers and responsibilities. This separation of powers helps to prevent any one branch of the federal government from becoming too powerful.

The Constitution also includes a number of specific provisions designed to balance federal power against state power. For example, the Tenth Amendment to the Constitution states that any powers not specifically granted to the federal government are reserved for the states. This provision helps to ensure that the federal government does not overstep its bounds and infringe on the powers of the states.

Another important provision of the Constitution that balances federal power against state power is the Supremacy Clause, which is found in Article VI of the Constitution. The Supremacy Clause establishes that the federal Constitution, laws passed by Congress, and treaties are the supreme law of the land. This provision helps to ensure that the federal government has the final say on certain issues, while also respecting the powers of the states.

The Supremacy Clause has been the subject of much debate and controversy over the years. Some have argued that it gives the federal government too much power and infringes on the rights of the states. Others have argued that it is necessary to ensure that the federal government can effectively address issues that affect the entire country.

One area in which the balance of power between the federal government and the states has been particularly contentious is in the realm of healthcare. The Affordable Care Act, also known as Obamacare, was a federal law designed to expand access to healthcare and reduce healthcare costs. However, many states opposed the law, arguing that it infringed on their rights and their ability to govern themselves.

The Supreme Court ultimately upheld the Affordable Care Act, but the case highlighted the ongoing tension between federal power and state power. While the federal government has the power to regulate healthcare under the Commerce Clause of the Constitution, some argued that the law went too far and infringed on the powers of the states.

Overall, the balance of power between the federal government and the states is a crucial part of American government and politics. The Constitution includes a number of provisions designed to ensure that the federal government does not become too powerful, while also recognizing the important role of the states in governing themselves. While there is often debate and controversy over the precise balance of power between the federal government and the states, this ongoing dialogue is an essential part of the American system of government.

The supremacy of the federal government over state governments

The supremacy of the federal government over state governments is a fundamental principle of the United States Constitution. This principle is enshrined in Article VI of the Constitution, which states that the Constitution, and the laws and treaties made under it, are the supreme law of the land. This means that federal law trumps state law in cases of conflict, and that state governments must comply with federal law.

The supremacy of the federal government was a controversial issue during the drafting of the Constitution. Some delegates believed that the federal government should have more power than the states, while others were concerned about the potential for federal tyranny. In the end, the framers of the Constitution struck a delicate balance between federal and state power, with the federal government having enumerated powers and the states retaining all other powers.

One of the key mechanisms for ensuring federal supremacy is the Supremacy Clause of Article VI. This clause establishes the Constitution, federal laws, and treaties as the supreme law of the land, and requires all state officials and judges to adhere to them. The Supremacy Clause has been used to settle a number of important legal disputes, including cases involving civil rights, environmental protection, and the regulation of commerce.

The Supremacy Clause has also been used to limit the power of state governments in certain areas. For example, the federal government has the power to regulate interstate commerce under the Commerce Clause of the Constitution, and this power has been used to strike down state laws that discriminate against out-of-state businesses. Similarly, the federal government's power to protect individual rights has been used to strike down state laws that infringe on those rights, such as laws that discriminate based on race or gender.

Another important mechanism for ensuring federal supremacy is the power of judicial review. The Supreme Court has the power to interpret the Constitution and to strike down any state law or action that is deemed unconstitutional. This power has been used to limit the power of state governments in a number of areas, including civil rights, abortion, and criminal justice.

Despite the principle of federal supremacy, there are still areas where state governments have significant power. For example, states have the power to regulate their own internal affairs, including matters of family law, property law, and criminal law. States also have the power to regulate certain areas of commerce that do not involve interstate activity, such as the sale of goods within the state.

However, even in areas where states have significant power, federal law still trumps state law in cases of conflict. For example, if a state law conflicts with a federal law on a matter of interstate commerce, the federal law will prevail. Similarly, if a state law conflicts with the Constitution or with a treaty, the state law will be struck down as unconstitutional.

The principle of federal supremacy has been the subject of much debate throughout American history. Some have argued that the federal government has overstepped its bounds and has infringed on the rights of the states, while others have argued that federal power is necessary to ensure the protection of individual rights and the promotion of national unity. Regardless of one's views on the matter, it is clear that the principle of federal supremacy is a central tenet of the American system of government, and is essential to the functioning of the federal system.

The supremacy of federal law over state law

The United States is a country that operates under a system of federalism, meaning power is divided between the federal government and state governments. However, in the event of a conflict between federal and state laws, the Constitution establishes that federal law is supreme. This principle, known as the supremacy clause, is outlined in Article VI of the Constitution.

The Constitution for Politicians

The supremacy clause states that "This Constitution, and the Laws of the United States which shall be made in Pursuance thereof; and all Treaties made, or which shall be made, under the Authority of the United States, shall be the supreme Law of the Land; and the Judges in every State shall be bound thereby, any Thing in the Constitution or Laws of any State to the Contrary notwithstanding."

In simpler terms, this means that if there is a conflict between a federal law and a state law, the federal law prevails. This ensures that there is a uniform standard across the country and prevents states from enacting laws that may conflict with the federal government's authority.

The supremacy of federal law over state law has been reinforced by a number of Supreme Court cases throughout history. One of the most well-known cases that addressed this issue was McCulloch v. Maryland in 1819. In this case, the Supreme Court established that the federal government had the power to create a national bank, and that state governments could not tax it. The Court reasoned that the Constitution granted certain implied powers to the federal government, and that these powers were supreme over state laws.

Another example of the supremacy of federal law over state law is the Civil Rights Act of 1964. This landmark legislation prohibited discrimination on the basis of race, color, religion, sex, or national origin in employment and public accommodations. Despite opposition from some states, the Supreme Court upheld the law's constitutionality and established that federal law was supreme over any conflicting state laws.

However, there are some limitations to the supremacy of federal law over state law. For example, federal laws must be within the scope of the federal government's enumerated powers in the Constitution. If a federal law exceeds the scope of these powers, it can be struck down as unconstitutional by the Supreme Court. Additionally, the Tenth Amendment to the Constitution reserves certain powers to the states, meaning that the federal government cannot encroach upon these powers.

One example of a conflict between federal and state law that has arisen in recent years is the legalization of marijuana. While some states have legalized marijuana for medical or recreational use, it remains illegal under federal law. This has created a tension between state and federal authorities, with some states arguing that the federal government should not interfere with their ability to regulate marijuana within their own borders.

Overall, the supremacy of federal law over state law is a critical aspect of the United States' system of government. It ensures that there is a uniform standard across the country and prevents states from enacting laws that may conflict with the federal government's authority. While there are limitations to this principle, it has been reinforced by a number of Supreme Court cases and remains an important part of American constitutional law.

Oaths of office for federal and state officials

Oaths of office for federal and state officials play a critical role in upholding the Constitution and ensuring that those who hold public office are committed to serving the best interests of their constituents. In this chapter, we will examine the purpose and significance of oaths of office, as well as the different oaths that federal and state officials must take.

I. Purpose and Significance of Oaths of Office

A. Definition and Purpose
An oath of office is a formal promise made by an individual who is assuming a position of public trust or authority. The purpose of the oath is to affirm the individual's commitment to uphold the Constitution and faithfully perform the duties of the office to the best of their ability. The oath of office is a critical tool in ensuring that those who hold public office are accountable to the people they serve and committed to upholding the principles of democratic governance.

B. Historical Significance

Oaths of office have a long history in American governance, dating back to the adoption of the Constitution in 1787. At the time, there was a widespread belief that a formal oath was necessary to bind public officials to the principles of the new government and to prevent corruption and abuse of power. The framers of the Constitution believed that a strong oath of office was essential to the success of the new republic, and they included an oath requirement in both the Constitution and the Bill of Rights.

C. Importance Today

Today, oaths of office remain a critical component of American governance. They serve as a reminder to public officials of the solemnity and importance of their duties and responsibilities, and they provide a means of holding officials accountable to the people they serve. Oaths of office are taken at every level of government, from the President of the United States to local school board members, and they play a key role in ensuring that government remains accountable and responsive to the needs of its citizens.

II. Federal Oaths of Office

A. The Presidential Oath of Office

The most well-known federal oath of office is the Presidential Oath of Office, which is required by the Constitution. The text of the oath is as follows: "I do solemnly swear (or affirm) that I will faithfully execute the office of President of the United States, and will to the best of my ability, preserve, protect and defend the Constitution of the United States." This oath is typically administered by the Chief Justice of the Supreme Court at the inauguration ceremony.

B. The Congressional Oath of Office

Members of Congress also take an oath of office, which is required by the Constitution. The text of the oath is as follows: "I do solemnly swear (or affirm) that I will support and defend the Constitution of the United States against all enemies, foreign and domestic; that I will bear true faith and allegiance to the same; that I take this obligation freely, without any mental reservation or purpose of evasion; and that I will well and faithfully discharge the duties of the office on which I am about to enter: So help me God." This oath is typically administered by the Speaker of the House or the Vice President of the United States.

C. Other Federal Oaths of Office

In addition to the Presidential and Congressional oaths of office, there are numerous other federal oaths of office, including those required for federal judges, members of the military, and executive branch officials. The specific wording of these oaths varies depending on the position, but all of them share a commitment to upholding the Constitution and serving the best interests of the American people.

III. State Oaths of Office

A. State Oaths of Office Generally

Like federal officials, state officials also take oaths of office when assuming their positions. The specifics of these oaths vary from state to state, but they all share a commitment to uphold the state and federal constitutions and faithfully discharge their duties.

B. State Oath of Office Examples

Here are some examples of state oaths of office:

California State Oath of Office
"I do solemnly swear (or affirm) that I will support and defend the Constitution of the United States and the Constitution of the State of California against all enemies, foreign and domestic; that I will bear true faith and allegiance to the Constitution of the United States and the Constitution of the State of California; that I take this obligation freely, without any mental reservation or purpose of evasion; and that I will well and faithfully discharge the duties upon which I am about to enter."

Texas State Oath of Office

"I, _____, do solemnly swear (or affirm), that I will faithfully execute the duties of the office of _____ of the State of Texas, and will to the best of my ability preserve, protect, and defend the Constitution and laws of the United States and of this State, so help me God."

New York State Oath of Office
"I do solemnly swear (or affirm) that I will support the Constitution of the United States, and the Constitution of the State of New York, and that I will faithfully discharge the duties of the office of _____ according to the best of my ability."

C. Importance of State Oaths of Office

State oaths of office are important because they ensure that state officials are committed to upholding both the state and federal constitutions. By taking an oath of office, state officials are affirming their dedication to serving the people and carrying out their duties with integrity and impartiality.

State officials have a wide range of responsibilities, from overseeing elections to enforcing state laws. It is crucial that they carry out these responsibilities in a way that is consistent with the principles of the state and federal constitutions, which protect the rights of individuals and limit the power of government.

D. Consequences of Violating State Oaths of Office

When state officials violate their oaths of office, they can face consequences ranging from removal from office to criminal charges. For example, in 2016, Alabama Chief Justice Roy Moore was suspended from his position for violating the state's ethical standards by ordering judges to ignore the U.S. Supreme Court's ruling legalizing same-sex marriage.

In addition to legal consequences, violating an oath of office can also damage an official's reputation and credibility. This can have long-term consequences, making it difficult for the official to gain the trust of the public and carry out their duties effectively.

E. Conclusion

State oaths of office are an important part of American government and ensure that state officials are committed to upholding the principles of the state and federal constitutions. By taking these oaths, officials are affirming their dedication to serving the people and carrying out their duties with integrity and impartiality. When officials violate these oaths, they can face legal and reputational consequences, underscoring the importance of upholding the oaths of office.

Fun examples of federal vs. state power struggles

The United States Constitution establishes a system of government that balances power between the federal government and the state governments. While this system has worked well for the most part, there have been numerous power struggles between the federal government and state governments throughout history. In this chapter, we will explore some fun and interesting examples of federal vs. state power struggles.

The Whiskey Rebellion

In 1791, the federal government passed a tax on distilled spirits, including whiskey. This tax was highly unpopular in western Pennsylvania, where farmers relied heavily on whiskey sales to supplement their income. In 1794, a group of farmers in western Pennsylvania rebelled against the tax, leading to what became known as the Whiskey Rebellion. President George Washington responded by sending a militia of 13,000 soldiers to put down the rebellion. The rebellion was quickly quashed, and the federal government's power to tax was reinforced.

The Nullification Crisis

The Constitution for Politicians

In the early 1830s, the state of South Carolina declared that it had the power to nullify federal laws that it deemed unconstitutional. This assertion of state power was in response to a federal tariff on imported goods that South Carolina believed was unfairly burdensome on the state's economy. President Andrew Jackson responded to South Carolina's nullification proclamation by threatening to use military force to enforce federal law. Ultimately, a compromise was reached, and the tariff was reduced, but the Nullification Crisis highlighted the ongoing tension between federal and state power.

Medical Marijuana

The federal government has long maintained that marijuana is a Schedule I drug under the Controlled Substances Act and is therefore illegal at the federal level. However, many states have passed laws legalizing medical marijuana, creating a conflict between state and federal law. This conflict has led to numerous legal battles and even raids by federal law enforcement on medical marijuana dispensaries in states where the drug is legal.

Same-Sex Marriage

In 2015, the Supreme Court ruled in the case of Obergefell v. Hodges that same-sex marriage is a constitutional right. This decision effectively legalized same-sex marriage throughout the United States. However, prior to this ruling, many states had passed their own laws defining marriage as being between one man and one woman. This led to a conflict between state and federal law, with some state officials refusing to issue marriage licenses to same-sex couples. The Supreme Court's decision ultimately resolved this conflict in favor of federal law.

Sanctuary Cities

The Constitution for Politicians

In recent years, some cities and states have declared themselves "sanctuary" jurisdictions, meaning that they will not cooperate with federal authorities in enforcing federal immigration laws. This has led to a conflict between these jurisdictions and the federal government, with the Trump administration threatening to withhold federal funding from sanctuary cities and the Biden administration taking a more lenient approach. This ongoing power struggle highlights the tension between federal and state power over immigration policy.

In conclusion, the United States Constitution established a system of government that balances power between the federal government and the state governments. However, this balance of power has not always been smooth, and there have been numerous power struggles between federal and state authorities throughout history. While some of these conflicts have been resolved through compromise and negotiation, others have required legal intervention from the courts. As the country continues to evolve, it is likely that we will see new examples of federal vs. state power struggles in the future.

In conclusion, the federal versus state power struggles that have occurred throughout American history demonstrate the complexity and challenges of the American political system. While the Constitution establishes a clear division of powers between the federal and state governments, conflicts can arise over the interpretation and exercise of those powers. The humorous and unexpected outcomes of some of these power struggles remind us that the relationship between the federal and state governments is constantly evolving and requires ongoing attention and adaptation. By understanding these power struggles, we can gain a deeper appreciation for the complexity and richness of American politics and governance.

CHAPTER 8: ARTICLE VII - RATIFICATION

- ❖ Article VII - Ratification
- ❖ The Break Down
- ❖ The process of ratifying the Constitution
- ❖ The historical context of the ratification process
- ❖ Number of states required for ratification
- ❖ Provisions for the establishment of the new government under the Constitution
- ❖ Humorous stories about early American politics

The Constitution for Politicians

Chapter 8 delves into several interesting aspects of early American politics, including the provisions for the establishment of the new government under the Constitution, the number of states required for ratification, and even some humorous stories from the time period. These topics help shed light on the challenges and triumphs of the early American political system, which laid the foundation for the stable and prosperous nation that we know today.

Article VII - Ratification

"The Ratification of the Conventions of nine States, shall be sufficient for the Establishment of this Constitution between the States so ratifying the Same."

This brief article outlines the process by which the Constitution would be officially ratified and put into effect. Specifically, it establishes that the Constitution would become binding between the states that had ratified it, but only after it had been ratified by at least nine of the thirteen original states. This threshold was met when New Hampshire became the ninth state to ratify the Constitution on June 21, 1788, paving the way for the new government to be established.

The Break Down

Article VII of the United States Constitution outlines the process for ratifying the Constitution. It states that the Constitution would go into effect once it had been ratified by nine of the thirteen original states. This provision ensured that the new government would have the legitimacy of being established by the people through their elected representatives. The ratification process began with the creation of the Constitution in 1787 and lasted until 1790, when the last two states, North Carolina and Rhode Island, finally ratified the document.

Harvard Law School's interpretation of Article VII of the U.S. Constitution is straightforward: it provides the procedure for ratifying the Constitution. The Article states that the Constitution will become effective once it has been ratified by nine of the thirteen states.

Harvard Law School also notes that the ratification process was not without its challenges. There were many debates and disagreements among the states about whether or not to ratify the Constitution, and some states only agreed to ratify it after certain amendments were added.

Overall, however, the ratification process was a critical step in establishing the new federal government and cementing the power of the Constitution as the supreme law of the land.

The Supreme Court has not issued any specific interpretation of Article VII of the Constitution, as it is a straightforward provision that simply outlines the requirements for ratification of the Constitution. However, the Court has recognized the significance of the ratification process and the legitimacy it gives to the Constitution as the fundamental law of the land.

In the case of Coleman v. Miller (1939), the Court addressed the question of whether the ratification of the Child Labor Amendment was still valid after several states had attempted to rescind their ratifications. The Court held that the question of whether a ratification is valid must be determined at the time it is made and that once the required number of states have ratified an amendment, the ratification is valid and cannot be revoked.

This decision affirmed the importance of the ratification process and the need for the states to carefully consider their actions before ratifying or attempting to rescind a ratification. It also reinforced the principle that the Constitution is a binding and enduring document, with the power to shape and govern the United States for generations to come.

The process of ratifying the Constitution

The United States Constitution is a fundamental document that governs the country's laws and system of government. It outlines the structure of the government and the rights of the people. However, before the Constitution could become the law of the land, it had to be ratified by the states. In this chapter, we will discuss the process of ratifying the Constitution.

When the Constitution was drafted in 1787, it needed to be approved by nine out of thirteen states to become law. The Framers of the Constitution knew that they would face significant opposition from the Anti-Federalists, who were skeptical of a strong central government. The Federalists, on the other hand, believed that a strong central government was necessary to maintain order and security.

The ratification process was a contentious and lengthy one, with debates and discussions taking place across the country. The process took over two years, from 1787 to 1789, and involved a series of conventions and debates.

The first step in the ratification process was for the Constitution to be submitted to the states for approval. The Constitution was sent to the Continental Congress, which was then responsible for sending it to the states. The states were given a copy of the Constitution, and each was asked to hold a convention to discuss and debate it.

The conventions were held in each of the thirteen states, with the exception of Rhode Island, which initially refused to participate. In some states, the conventions were open to the public, while in others, only elected officials were allowed to attend. The debates in these conventions were heated, and both the Federalists and the Anti-Federalists presented their arguments.

The Federalists argued that the Constitution was necessary to provide a strong central government that could maintain order and protect the rights of the people. They also argued that the Constitution provided a system of checks and balances to prevent any one branch of government from becoming too powerful.

The Anti-Federalists, on the other hand, argued that the Constitution would create a government that was too powerful and could easily abuse its power. They also argued that the Constitution did not do enough to protect the rights of the people.

Despite these disagreements, the conventions eventually began to vote on whether to ratify the Constitution. In order to be ratified, the Constitution needed to be approved by nine out of thirteen states.

The first state to ratify the Constitution was Delaware, which did so on December 7, 1787. Pennsylvania and New Jersey quickly followed, with Pennsylvania ratifying on December 12 and New Jersey on December 18. By the end of 1787, three states had ratified the Constitution.

In 1788, the pace of ratification picked up, with five states ratifying in quick succession. Georgia, Connecticut, Massachusetts, Maryland, and South Carolina all ratified the Constitution in early 1788.

The final states to ratify the Constitution were New Hampshire and Virginia. New Hampshire ratified the Constitution on June 21, 1788, and Virginia ratified it on June 25, 1788. With the ratification of Virginia, the Constitution had been approved by nine states and became law.

Rhode Island was the only state that did not ratify the Constitution initially. The state held a referendum in 1788, but it was defeated by a wide margin. Rhode Island eventually ratified the Constitution in 1790, after the new federal government threatened to cut off trade with the state.

In conclusion, the ratification process was a significant moment in the history of the United States. It was a time when the people of the country came together to debate and discuss the Constitution, and ultimately decide its fate. The process was contentious, and the debates were heated, but in the end, the Constitution was ratified and became the law of the land. The ratification process also set a precedent for future amendments to the Constitution and emphasized the importance of the people's voice in shaping the government.

The ratification process was a testament to the democratic ideals that the Founding Fathers held so dear. It was a process that allowed for dissenting opinions and debate, but ultimately resulted in a unified decision to move forward with a new form of government.

Today, the Constitution remains the cornerstone of American democracy and serves as a model for other nations around the world. Its principles of individual rights, limited government, and checks and balances have stood the test of time and continue to shape the political landscape of the United States.

It is important to remember the significance of the ratification process and the role it played in shaping the country we live in today. The process serves as a reminder that democracy is not a stagnant concept, but rather a dynamic one that requires constant evaluation and adaptation to meet the needs of a changing society.

In the end, the ratification process gave birth to a nation that has become a beacon of hope and freedom for people around the world. It is a testament to the power of democracy and the ability of a people to come together to create a government that represents their interests and protects their rights.

The historical context of the ratification process

The ratification process of the Constitution took place during a time of great political and social upheaval in the newly-formed United States. The country was still recovering from the Revolutionary War and struggling to establish a stable government that could effectively govern the diverse and rapidly-growing nation.

The Articles of Confederation, the first attempt at a national government, had proven to be ineffective in addressing the needs of the country. The government had limited powers and lacked the ability to raise taxes or regulate trade between states. This led to economic instability and political tension between the states.

The Constitutional Convention was called in 1787 to address these issues and draft a new constitution that would create a stronger, more centralized government. The delegates who attended the convention were some of the most prominent political figures of the time, including George Washington, James Madison, and Benjamin Franklin.

The debates at the convention were intense, and the delegates had to navigate complex issues such as representation, taxation, and the balance of power between the federal government and the states. After four months of negotiation and compromise, the delegates produced a final draft of the Constitution that they believed would create a more perfect union.

However, the proposed Constitution faced significant opposition from both anti-federalists and some of the states themselves. Many feared that the new government would become too powerful and trample on individual rights and liberties.

The debates over the ratification of the Constitution were heated and passionate, with both sides presenting compelling arguments. The anti-federalists, led by figures such as Patrick Henry and Samuel Adams, argued that the Constitution gave too much power to the federal government and threatened the sovereignty of the states. They also argued that the lack of a Bill of Rights would leave citizens vulnerable to government abuse.

On the other side, the federalists, led by figures such as Alexander Hamilton and James Madison, argued that a strong federal government was necessary to provide stability and protect the rights of citizens. They believed that the Constitution contained sufficient checks and balances to prevent abuses of power and that a Bill of Rights was unnecessary.

The ratification process was a complex and lengthy one, with each state holding its own convention to debate and vote on the proposed Constitution. In order for the Constitution to become law, it needed to be ratified by nine of the thirteen states.

The first state to ratify the Constitution was Delaware, followed by Pennsylvania and New Jersey. However, the road to ratification was not without obstacles. In Massachusetts, the Constitution faced significant opposition, with many fearing that it would erode individual liberties. In order to secure ratification, the federalists agreed to support a Bill of Rights, which would be added to the Constitution after ratification.

In Virginia, the ratification debates were particularly contentious, with both sides presenting compelling arguments. The federalists ultimately prevailed, and Virginia became the tenth state to ratify the Constitution.

New York, another important state, was also divided over the Constitution. The anti-federalists argued that the Constitution gave too much power to the federal government and lacked sufficient protections for individual liberties. In order to secure ratification, the federalists agreed to support a Bill of Rights and to address specific concerns raised by the anti-federalists.

North Carolina and Rhode Island were the final states to ratify the Constitution, with both states initially rejecting it before eventually ratifying it in 1789 and 1790, respectively.

In conclusion, the ratification process was a crucial moment in the history of the United States. It was a time of great political and social upheaval, and the debates over the Constitution were heated and passionate. Ultimately, the Constitution was ratified, and it became the supreme law of the land, laying the foundation for the stable and prosperous nation that we know today. The ratification process was a testament to the resilience and determination of the American people, and it reflected the unique historical context in which it took place.

The ratification process was shaped by a complex web of factors, including the legacy of the American Revolution, the failures of the Articles of Confederation, and the competing interests of the various states. It was also influenced by the ideas and philosophies of the Enlightenment, which emphasized the importance of reason, liberty, and individual rights.

The ratification debates were characterized by a diverse range of opinions and viewpoints. Some delegates, such as the Federalists, favored a strong central government and believed that the Constitution provided the best framework for achieving this goal. Others, such as the Anti-Federalists, were concerned about the potential for tyranny and argued for greater protection of individual rights and state sovereignty.

The ratification process was also shaped by the personalities and political agendas of the delegates themselves. Many of the delegates were experienced politicians and statesmen, while others were relatively unknown figures who were thrust into the national spotlight. Some delegates, such as Alexander Hamilton and James Madison, played key roles in shaping the Constitution and advocating for its ratification. Others, such as Patrick Henry and George Mason, opposed the Constitution and argued for its rejection.

Throughout the ratification process, both sides employed a wide range of tactics to win support for their positions. The Federalists, for example, wrote a series of influential essays known as The Federalist Papers, which sought to explain and defend the Constitution. The Anti-Federalists, meanwhile, distributed pamphlets and held public meetings to voice their opposition to the Constitution.

Ultimately, the ratification process was a triumph of compromise and negotiation. Despite their many differences, the delegates were able to come together and agree on a Constitution that provided a framework for a strong and stable federal government while also protecting the rights and interests of individual states and citizens.

In the end, the ratification process established the Constitution as the supreme law of the land, and set the stage for the development of a strong and stable federal government. It was a moment of great importance in the history of the United States, and it continues to shape our political and social landscape to this day.

In conclusion, the historical context of the ratification process provides important insights into the challenges and complexities of establishing a strong and stable federal government. The process was shaped by a wide range of factors, including the legacy of the American Revolution, the failures of the Articles of Confederation, and the competing interests of the various states. It was also influenced by the ideas and philosophies of the Enlightenment, and characterized by a diverse range of opinions and viewpoints. Ultimately, however, the ratification process was a testament to the resilience and determination of the American people, and it laid the foundation for the stable and prosperous nation that we know today.

Number of states required for ratification

When the Constitution was first drafted, it faced a significant hurdle in being ratified by the states. The Constitution represented a significant departure from the Articles of Confederation, which had been the governing document of the United States since its inception. As a result, the ratification process required a significant amount of debate and compromise before the Constitution could be adopted as the supreme law of the land.

One of the key issues that arose during the ratification process was the question of how many states would be required to ratify the Constitution. The Constitution itself did not provide a clear answer to this question, leaving it up to the states to decide. This led to a significant amount of debate and negotiation among the states as they sought to determine the threshold for ratification.

Ultimately, the decision was made to require the approval of nine of the thirteen states for the Constitution to be ratified. This decision was made in the context of a heated debate over the role of the federal government, and the extent to which it should be able to wield power over the states.

At the time, there were concerns that requiring too many states to ratify the Constitution would make it difficult for smaller states to have a voice in the process. Some argued that requiring only a simple majority of states to ratify the Constitution would be more fair and democratic. However, others argued that the Constitution represented a fundamental change in the nature of the federal government, and that a higher threshold for ratification was necessary to ensure that the states retained their autonomy and independence.

The Constitution for Politicians

Ultimately, the decision to require nine states to ratify the Constitution proved to be a wise one. The nine states that ratified the Constitution represented a diverse cross-section of the country, including both large and small states, as well as states from different regions and with different economic interests. This helped to ensure that the Constitution was seen as a legitimate governing document that represented the interests of the entire country, rather than just a small group of powerful states.

In addition to the nine states that ratified the Constitution, there were four states that initially rejected it: North Carolina, Rhode Island, New York, and Virginia. However, over time, these states were persuaded to ratify the Constitution, either through amendments that addressed their concerns or through other forms of political pressure.

The ratification of the Constitution was a critical moment in the history of the United States. It represented a significant departure from the Articles of Confederation, which had proven to be an ineffective governing document. The Constitution provided a framework for a stronger, more centralized government, while also protecting the rights and interests of individual states.

Today, the requirement for nine states to ratify an amendment to the Constitution remains in place. This has helped to ensure that any changes to the Constitution are made with the support of a significant portion of the country, rather than being imposed by a small group of powerful states.

In conclusion, the decision to require nine states to ratify the Constitution was a critical moment in the history of the United States. It helped to ensure that the Constitution was seen as a legitimate governing document that represented the interests of the entire country, rather than just a small group of powerful states. The requirement for nine states to ratify an amendment remains in place to this day, and it continues to be an important safeguard against hasty and ill-considered changes to the Constitution.

Provisions for the establishment of the new government under the Constitution

The United States Constitution is the supreme law of the land, providing the framework for the federal government's operation and defining the relationship between the government and the people. When the Constitution was ratified in 1788, it established a new government, replacing the previous Articles of Confederation. This new government was based on the principle of separation of powers, with a strong executive, a bicameral legislature, and an independent judiciary. In this chapter, we will explore the provisions for the establishment of this new government under the Constitution.

I. The Three Branches of Government

Under the Constitution, the federal government is divided into three branches: the legislative, executive, and judicial branches. This separation of powers ensures that no one branch has too much power, and each branch serves as a check on the others.

A. The Legislative Branch

The legislative branch, also known as Congress, is responsible for making the laws of the land. It is composed of two chambers: the Senate and the House of Representatives. The Senate has two members from each state, while the number of representatives in the House is based on each state's population.

B. The Executive Branch

The executive branch is responsible for enforcing the laws of the land. It is headed by the President of the United States, who is elected by the people every four years. The President has the power to veto legislation passed by Congress, which can then be overridden by a two-thirds vote in both the House and Senate.

C. The Judicial Branch

The Constitution for Politicians

The judicial branch is responsible for interpreting the laws of the land. It is composed of the Supreme Court and lower federal courts. The President nominates Supreme Court justices, who must then be confirmed by the Senate.

II. Powers and Limitations of the Federal Government

The Constitution grants the federal government specific powers, but it also places limitations on those powers to protect the rights of the people.

A. Enumerated Powers

The Constitution grants the federal government certain enumerated powers, such as the power to regulate commerce between states, declare war, and establish a uniform system of naturalization.

B. Reserved Powers

The Constitution reserves certain powers for the states, such as the power to establish schools and regulate intrastate commerce.

C. Bill of Rights

The Bill of Rights, the first ten amendments to the Constitution, guarantees certain individual rights and protections, such as the freedom of speech, religion, and the press, and the right to a fair and speedy trial.

III. Constitutional Amendments

The Constitution also provides for the amendment process, which allows for changes to be made to the document as the country and its needs evolve over time. This process requires a two-thirds vote of both the House and Senate, or a convention called for by two-thirds of the states, followed by ratification by three-fourths of the states.

IV. Supremacy of the Constitution

The Constitution is the supreme law of the land, meaning that all other laws and actions must be in accordance with its provisions. This ensures that the government operates within the limits established by the Constitution and protects the rights of the people.

V. Conclusion

The provisions for the establishment of the new government under the Constitution were designed to create a balanced system of power that would protect the rights of the people while ensuring effective governance. The separation of powers, enumerated and reserved powers, and the Bill of Rights are all essential components of this system. The Constitution has proven to be a durable and adaptable document, able to withstand the challenges of time and changes in society. The Constitution is the foundation of the United States government, and it remains the bedrock of American democracy to this day.

Humorous stories about early American politics

The history of American politics is full of fascinating and often humorous stories. From political rivalries to unconventional campaign tactics, early American politics was no exception. Here are a few humorous stories about early American politics that highlight the quirks and idiosyncrasies of our nation's founders.

The Great Cheese

In 1801, the town of Cheshire, Massachusetts sent a massive, 1,235-pound cheese to President Thomas Jefferson as a gift. The cheese was made from the milk of 900 cows and was intended to promote the dairy industry in the region. However, Jefferson had no idea what to do with such a large and unwieldy gift. After storing the cheese in the White House for over a year, he finally decided to share it with the public at a Fourth of July celebration in 1802.

Aaron Burr's Dueling Grounds

Aaron Burr, the third Vice President of the United States, was notorious for his involvement in a deadly duel with Alexander Hamilton in 1804. However, Burr was also known for his peculiar hobby of creating dueling grounds. He built a dueling ground in Weehawken, New Jersey, and would often take visitors there to show off his skills with a pistol. Burr even went so far as to issue a challenge to President James Madison to a duel, which was promptly ignored.

The New York Gubernatorial Election of 1804

The New York gubernatorial election of 1804 was one of the most bizarre and contentious in American history. The incumbent governor, George Clinton, was challenged by Aaron Burr, who had just killed Alexander Hamilton in a duel. The election quickly turned into a mudslinging contest, with both candidates hurling insults and accusations at each other. In the end, Clinton won the election, but not before Burr accused him of being a "political hypocrite" and a "demi-republican."

The Election of 1824

The election of 1824 was one of the most controversial in American history. The race was between four candidates: John Quincy Adams, Andrew Jackson, Henry Clay, and William Crawford. Jackson won the popular vote but fell short of the necessary number of electoral votes to win the presidency. In the end, the decision was made by the House of Representatives, which elected Adams as president. Jackson and his supporters were furious, and accused Adams of making a "corrupt bargain" with Henry Clay.

The Battle of the Hickory Cane

The Battle of the Hickory Cane was a political brawl that took place in the halls of Congress in 1838. The incident began when Representative William Graves of Kentucky accused Representative

Jonathan Cilley of Maine of being a liar. Cilley demanded an apology, but Graves refused. The two men agreed to settle the matter with a duel, but Cilley was killed before the duel could take place. The incident sparked a national debate over the practice of dueling and led to the passage of anti-dueling laws in several states.

These humorous stories from early American politics remind us that politics has always been a colorful and sometimes strange world. From giant cheeses to deadly duels, our nation's founders were never dull, and their quirks and idiosyncrasies have left an indelible mark on American history.

CHAPTER 9: BILL OF RIGHTS

❖ Introduction
❖ The First Ten Amendments to the Constitution
❖ Importance of Individual Rights and Liberties
❖ Funny Examples of How the Bill of Rights is Applied Today
❖ Conclusion

Introduction
➤ Brief overview of the Bill of Rights
➤ Importance of individual rights and liberties in American society

The Bill of Rights is one of the most significant documents in American history. It is a testament to the importance of individual rights and liberties in American society, and it serves as a bulwark against the encroachment of government power. The Bill of Rights consists of the first ten amendments to the United States Constitution, which were ratified in 1791. In this chapter, we will provide a brief overview of the Bill of Rights and examine the importance of individual rights and liberties in American society.

The Bill of Rights: A Brief Overview

The Constitution for Politicians

The Bill of Rights is a collection of ten amendments to the United States Constitution, which were ratified on December 15, 1791. The amendments were proposed by James Madison, who was instrumental in drafting the Constitution itself. The Bill of Rights was added to the Constitution in order to address concerns about individual rights and liberties, which were not sufficiently protected by the original Constitution.

The Bill of Rights contains ten amendments, each of which deals with a different aspect of individual rights and liberties. The first amendment guarantees freedom of speech, religion, and the press, as well as the right to assemble and petition the government. The second amendment guarantees the right to bear arms. The third amendment prohibits the government from forcing citizens to quarter soldiers in their homes. The fourth amendment protects citizens from unreasonable searches and seizures. The fifth amendment guarantees the right to due process of law and protection against self-incrimination. The sixth amendment guarantees the right to a fair trial. The seventh amendment guarantees the right to a trial by jury in civil cases. The eighth amendment prohibits excessive bail and fines, as well as cruel and unusual punishment. The ninth amendment states that the enumeration of certain rights in the Constitution shall not be construed to deny or disparage other rights retained by the people. The tenth amendment reserves to the states or to the people all powers not delegated to the federal government by the Constitution.

The Importance of Individual Rights and Liberties in American Society

The United States was founded on the principle that individual rights and liberties are of paramount importance. The Declaration of Independence, which was issued in 1776, states that all men are created equal and are endowed by their Creator with certain unalienable rights, including the right to life, liberty, and the pursuit of happiness. These ideas were enshrined in the Constitution, which was designed to limit the power of the federal government and to protect individual rights and liberties.

The Bill of Rights is an essential part of this protection. It guarantees a number of important rights, including the freedom of speech, religion, and the press, the right to bear arms, and the right to a fair trial. These rights are fundamental to American society, and they are essential for maintaining a free and democratic society. Without these rights, the government could easily become oppressive and tyrannical, trampling on the rights and liberties of individual citizens.

The Bill of Rights has been used to protect individual rights and liberties in a number of important ways throughout American history. For example, the First Amendment has been used to protect the rights of protesters, journalists, and others to express their views without fear of government reprisal. The Second Amendment has been used to protect the right of citizens to own guns for self-defense and other lawful purposes. The Fourth Amendment has been used to prevent the government from engaging in unreasonable searches and seizures. And the Fifth Amendment has been used to protect citizens against self-incrimination and to ensure that they receive due process of law.

In addition to protecting individual rights and liberties, the Bill of Rights also serves as a bulwark against government tyranny. It sets limits on the power of the federal government, and it ensures that individual citizens have a means of resisting government oppression. The Bill of Rights is therefore an essential component of American democracy, helping to safeguard the freedoms and rights of citizens.

The Bill of Rights is often hailed as one of the greatest accomplishments in American history. It was added to the Constitution in response to fears that the federal government might abuse its power and infringe upon the rights of individuals. The Bill of Rights establishes basic protections for individual liberties such as freedom of speech, religion, and the press, as well as the right to bear arms and the right to a fair trial.

The Bill of Rights reflects the belief of the Founding Fathers that individual rights are an essential component of democracy. Without these rights, the government could become a tool of oppression, and citizens could be subjected to arbitrary arrests, imprisonment, or even execution without a fair trial. The Bill of Rights ensures that individual freedoms are protected and that the government is held accountable to its citizens.

The Bill of Rights is an integral part of American culture, and it has shaped the nation's values and identity. The protections it provides have become the bedrock of American democracy, and they have been fiercely defended by citizens throughout the country's history.

As we move forward, it is essential to remember the importance of the Bill of Rights and to continue to defend the freedoms and rights it enshrines. In doing so, we can uphold the legacy of the Founding Fathers and continue to build a more just and equitable society for all.

The First Ten Amendments to the Constitution

> ➢ Overview of each amendment and its purpose
> ➢ Historical context and events that led to their creation

The First Ten Amendments to the United States Constitution, also known as the Bill of Rights, were added to the Constitution in 1791 to protect individual liberties and to limit the power of the federal government.

Here is the full text for each of the ten amendments:

Amendment 1: Freedom of religion, freedom of speech, freedom of the press, the right to assemble, and the right to petition the government.

Amendment 2: The right to bear arms.

Amendment 3: Protection from quartering of troops in private homes.

Amendment 4: Protection against unreasonable searches and seizures.

Amendment 5: Protection of the rights of the accused, including the right to a grand jury, protection from double jeopardy, and the right to due process of law.

Amendment 6: The right to a fair and speedy trial, the right to an impartial jury, the right to be informed of the charges against oneself, the right to confront witnesses, and the right to have legal representation.

Amendment 7: The right to a trial by jury in civil cases.

Amendment 8: Protection against excessive bail and fines, and against cruel and unusual punishment.

Amendment 9: Protection of unenumerated rights retained by the people.

Amendment 10: Powers not delegated to the federal government by the Constitution, nor prohibited by it to the states, are reserved to the states or to the people.

Overview of each amendment and its purpose

The first ten amendments to the Constitution, collectively known as the Bill of Rights, were added in 1791 in order to protect individual rights and limit the power of the federal government. In this chapter, we will provide an overview of each amendment and its purpose.

Amendment 1: Freedom of Religion, Speech, Press, Assembly, and Petition

The First Amendment protects the fundamental rights of freedom of religion, freedom of speech, freedom of the press, the right to assemble, and the right to petition the government for a redress of grievances. This amendment is critical for the functioning of a free society, as it allows individuals to express themselves without fear of government reprisal. It also guarantees the separation of church and state, ensuring that no single religion is given preferential treatment by the government.

Amendment 2: Right to Bear Arms

The Second Amendment protects the right of individuals to bear arms. It was added to the Constitution to ensure that citizens would be able to defend themselves against a potentially tyrannical government, as well as to allow for the formation of a well-regulated militia.

Amendment 3: Quartering of Troops

The Third Amendment prohibits the government from requiring citizens to quarter (house) soldiers in their homes without their consent. This amendment was added in response to the abuses of British soldiers who were quartered in colonists' homes without their consent during the Revolutionary War.

Amendment 4: Search and Seizure

The Fourth Amendment protects citizens from unreasonable searches and seizures by the government. It requires that the government obtain a warrant before conducting a search or seizure, and that the warrant be based on probable cause.

Amendment 5: Due Process, Double Jeopardy, and Self-Incrimination

The Fifth Amendment protects citizens' rights in criminal proceedings. It guarantees the right to due process of law, protection against double jeopardy (being tried twice for the same crime), and the right to remain silent (protection against self-incrimination).

Amendment 6: Right to a Fair Trial

The Sixth Amendment guarantees the right to a fair and speedy trial by an impartial jury, the right to be informed of the charges against oneself, the right to confront witnesses, and the right to have legal counsel.

Amendment 7: Trial by Jury

The Seventh Amendment guarantees the right to a trial by jury in certain civil cases. This right is critical for ensuring that disputes between citizens are decided fairly and impartially.

Amendment 8: Cruel and Unusual Punishment

The Eighth Amendment prohibits the government from imposing cruel and unusual punishment on citizens. It also prohibits excessive fines and bail, ensuring that punishment is proportional to the crime committed.

Amendment 9: Rights Retained by the People

The Ninth Amendment states that the enumeration of certain rights in the Constitution shall not be construed to deny or disparage other rights retained by the people. This amendment is important because it acknowledges that the list of rights contained in the Constitution is not exhaustive, and that citizens have other rights beyond those explicitly listed.

Amendment 10: Powers Reserved to the States

The Tenth Amendment reserves powers not delegated to the federal government to the states or to the people. This amendment was added to ensure that the federal government would not become too powerful and that individual states would retain a degree of autonomy.

In conclusion, the Bill of Rights is a cornerstone of American democracy, protecting individual rights and limiting the power of the federal government. Each amendment serves a critical purpose, and together they provide a framework for a free and just society.

Historical context and events that led to their creation

The Bill of Rights is a crucial part of the United States Constitution that protects individual liberties and limits the power of the government. But where did the idea for the Bill of Rights come from, and what historical events led to its creation? In this chapter, we will explore the historical context and events that led to the creation of the Bill of Rights.

The Roots of the Bill of Rights

The concept of individual rights and liberties has deep roots in English common law and political philosophy. The Magna Carta, signed in 1215, established the principle that the king was subject to the law and could not act arbitrarily. Over the centuries, this principle was expanded upon by legal scholars and philosophers, such as John Locke, who argued that individuals had certain natural rights that were inherent and could not be taken away by the government.

In the American colonies, these ideas of individual rights and liberties were central to the colonial charters and colonial law. The colonists believed that they had certain rights as Englishmen, including the right to a trial by jury, the right to be free from arbitrary arrest, and the right to due process of law. These rights were enshrined in colonial charters and were fiercely protected by the colonists.

The Events that Led to the Bill of Rights

The American Revolution marked a turning point in the struggle for individual rights and liberties. The colonists rebelled against what they saw as the oppressive rule of the British government, and in 1776, they declared their independence from Great Britain. The Declaration of Independence, written by Thomas Jefferson, proclaimed that all men were created equal and had certain inalienable rights, including the right to life, liberty, and the pursuit of happiness.

The Constitution for Politicians

After the American Revolution, the newly formed states began to write their own constitutions. Many of these constitutions included bills of rights, which listed specific rights and protections for individual citizens. These bills of rights were seen as essential safeguards against government tyranny, and they helped to establish the idea that individual rights were fundamental and could not be taken away by the government.

However, the Articles of Confederation, which served as the first national constitution, did not include a bill of rights. The Articles of Confederation gave the federal government very little power, and it was largely left up to the individual states to protect the rights of their citizens. This led to a patchwork of laws and protections across the country, and it became clear that a stronger national government was needed to ensure that individual rights were protected.

The Constitutional Convention and the Debate over the Bill of Rights

In 1787, a convention was called in Philadelphia to address the weaknesses of the Articles of Confederation. This convention resulted in the drafting of the United States Constitution, which established a stronger federal government and a system of checks and balances to prevent the abuse of power.

However, the Constitution did not include a bill of rights. This was a point of contention for many delegates at the Constitutional Convention, who believed that a bill of rights was necessary to protect individual liberties. Anti-Federalists, who opposed the Constitution, argued that without a bill of rights, the federal government would be free to infringe upon individual liberties and become as tyrannical as the British government had been.

In order to secure the ratification of the Constitution, Federalists, who supported the Constitution, promised that a bill of rights would be added to the Constitution after it was ratified. This promise was instrumental in securing the support of many Anti-Federalists, and the Constitution was ratified in 1788.

The Creation and Ratification of the Bill of Rights

In 1789, James Madison, a Federalist and future president, introduced a series of amendments to the Constitution Madison's original proposal contained 19 amendments, but Congress eventually reduced the number to 12. Ten of these amendments were ratified by the required number of states on December 15, 1791, and became known as the Bill of Rights.

The drafting and ratification of the Bill of Rights was not without controversy. While some anti-Federalists argued that the Constitution did not adequately protect individual rights and liberties, others, including Alexander Hamilton, believed that a Bill of Rights was unnecessary. Hamilton argued that the Constitution already provided sufficient protections for individual liberties and that adding a Bill of Rights would only serve to limit the power of the federal government.

However, the anti-Federalists were successful in their efforts to add a Bill of Rights to the Constitution. They argued that a Bill of Rights was necessary to protect the people from the potential abuses of the federal government, and their arguments ultimately won the day.

The Bill of Rights was not only a product of political compromise and negotiation, but it was also influenced by the events of the time. One of the key events that influenced the drafting of the Bill of Rights was the American Revolution. The colonists' struggle for independence from Great Britain was based on a desire for greater individual liberty and freedom from government tyranny. The Bill of Rights was seen as a way to ensure that the new federal government did not become tyrannical like the British government that the colonists had rebelled against.

Additionally, the Bill of Rights was influenced by the experiences of the states. Many states had already adopted their own bills of rights, and these documents served as a model for the federal Bill of Rights. For example, the Virginia Declaration of Rights, written by George Mason in 1776, included many of the same provisions that would later appear in the federal Bill of Rights.

The Bill of Rights was also influenced by the fears and concerns of the time. Many Americans were concerned that the federal government would become too powerful and would use that power to trample on individual liberties. The Bill of Rights was seen as a way to limit the power of the federal government and protect individual rights and liberties.

In conclusion, the drafting and ratification of the Bill of Rights was a complex and controversial process. It was influenced by the events of the time, including the American Revolution and the experiences of the states, as well as the fears and concerns of the American people. Ultimately, the Bill of Rights became an essential part of the Constitution, protecting individual rights and liberties and ensuring that the federal government would not become tyrannical.

Importance of Individual Rights and Liberties

> ➢ How the Bill of Rights protects individual rights and liberties
> ➢ Examples of how these rights have been upheld in American history

Individual rights and liberties have been a cornerstone of American society since the country's founding. The United States was established as a nation based on the principles of democracy, freedom, and justice for all, and the protection of individual rights and liberties is essential to realizing these ideals. The Bill of Rights, the first ten amendments to the Constitution, outlines specific individual rights that the government is obligated to protect. In this chapter, we will explore the importance of individual rights and liberties in American society.

First, let's define what we mean by "individual rights and liberties." These are the rights and freedoms that individuals possess simply by virtue of being human. They include the right to free speech, religion, assembly, and the press, as well as the right to bear arms, a fair trial, and freedom from unreasonable searches and seizures. These rights are considered fundamental because they are essential to the protection of individual dignity, autonomy, and well-being. They allow individuals to live their lives without fear of government oppression or persecution.

The importance of individual rights and liberties in American society can be traced back to the country's founding. The American Revolution was fought, in part, to secure individual liberties that the colonists believed were being violated by the British government. The Declaration of Independence, which declared the United States' independence from Great Britain, asserted that all men are created equal and endowed with certain inalienable rights, including the rights to life, liberty, and the pursuit of happiness.

After the Revolutionary War, the framers of the Constitution sought to create a government that would protect individual rights and liberties while also maintaining order and stability. However, many feared that the new government could become tyrannical and violate individual rights, as had happened under British rule. To address these concerns, the Bill of Rights was added to the Constitution as a safeguard against government overreach.

The Bill of Rights outlines specific individual rights and liberties that the government is obligated to protect. For example, the First Amendment protects freedom of speech, religion, assembly, and the press. The Second Amendment protects the right to bear arms. The Fourth Amendment protects against unreasonable searches and seizures, and the Fifth Amendment protects the right to a fair trial and due process of law. These are just a few examples of the many individual rights and liberties protected by the Bill of Rights.

The importance of these rights cannot be overstated. They are essential to the protection of individual freedom, autonomy, and dignity. Without them, individuals could be subject to government oppression and persecution, as happened under British rule. The Bill of Rights provides a bulwark against government tyranny and ensures that individuals have a means of resisting government overreach.

Individual rights and liberties also play a crucial role in promoting social and political progress. They allow individuals to express dissenting opinions, to advocate for change, and to challenge the status quo. Without these rights, progress and innovation could be stifled, and societies could become stagnant and oppressive.

However, protecting individual rights and liberties is not always easy. In times of national crisis, such as war or terrorism, there is often pressure to curtail individual freedoms in the name of national security. This tension between security and liberty is a longstanding one, and it has led to many debates and controversies over the years. However, it is important to remember that protecting individual rights and liberties is essential to maintaining a free and democratic society. Without these rights, democracy cannot exist, and individuals cannot be truly free.

In conclusion, individual rights and liberties are essential to the protection of individual freedom, autonomy, and dignity. They are a cornerstone of American society and have been since the country's founding. The Bill of Rights outlines specific individual rights that the government is obligated to protect, and it serves as a bulwark against government tyranny. Protecting these rights is essential to maintaining a free and democratic society, and it is important for individuals to remain vigilant in ensuring that their rights are not infringed upon.

Throughout history, there have been numerous examples of governments and leaders who have attempted to suppress individual rights and liberties, often with disastrous consequences. The Founding Fathers were well aware of this danger and took great care to enshrine individual rights and liberties in the Constitution and the Bill of Rights. They understood that without such protections, the government would have unchecked power over its citizens, leading to oppression, tyranny, and the erosion of democracy.

The Bill of Rights protects a wide range of individual rights, including the freedom of speech, religion, and the press, as well as the right to bear arms, due process, and equal protection under the law. These rights are not absolute, and they may be limited under certain circumstances, such as when they conflict with the public good or the rights of others. However, any such limitations must be carefully weighed against the potential harm to individual freedom and autonomy.

Moreover, the protection of individual rights and liberties is not only essential to maintaining a free and democratic society, but it is also crucial to fostering innovation, creativity, and progress. When individuals are free to express themselves, pursue their passions, and exercise their autonomy, they are more likely to come up with new and innovative ideas that can benefit society as a whole.

For example, the freedom of speech and the press have been instrumental in promoting scientific discovery, artistic expression, and political discourse. Without these freedoms, many of the world's greatest achievements and advancements would not have been possible.

Similarly, the right to bear arms has played a critical role in protecting individual autonomy and safety. While some may argue that this right is outdated in modern society, it remains a vital protection against government oppression and individual threats to safety.

In recent years, there have been concerns that the protection of individual rights and liberties is under threat. In particular, there has been a growing trend towards government surveillance, censorship, and restrictions on free speech and the press. These actions pose a significant threat to individual freedom and autonomy, and they must be vigorously opposed by those who value these fundamental rights.

The protection of individual rights and liberties is not only a legal and political issue but also a moral one. It is a recognition of the inherent value and dignity of each individual, and it is a recognition that individuals should be free to live their lives as they see fit, as long as they do not harm others.

In conclusion, the protection of individual rights and liberties is a cornerstone of American society and is essential to maintaining a free and democratic society. The Bill of Rights outlines specific individual rights that the government is obligated to protect, and it serves as a bulwark against government tyranny. Protecting these rights is essential to ensuring that individuals are free to pursue their passions, express themselves, and live their lives as they see fit. As such, it is important for individuals to remain vigilant in ensuring that their rights are not infringed upon and to vigorously oppose any actions that threaten the protection of these fundamental rights.

How the Bill of Rights protects individual rights and liberties

The Bill of Rights is a crucial component of the United States Constitution. Its ten amendments guarantee individual rights and freedoms, and they are designed to prevent the government from abusing its power. In this chapter, we will explore how the Bill of Rights protects individual rights and liberties in America.

First Amendment

The First Amendment is perhaps the most well-known of all the amendments. It guarantees several essential individual rights, including freedom of speech, religion, press, assembly, and the right to petition the government for redress of grievances. These rights are essential to maintaining a free and democratic society, as they allow individuals to express themselves and advocate for change without fear of government retribution.

The First Amendment has been tested time and again throughout American history. From the Alien and Sedition Acts of 1798 to the Supreme Court case of Tinker v. Des Moines Independent Community School District in 1969, which ruled that students have the right to express their political beliefs in school, the First Amendment has been the subject of countless debates and legal battles. But through it all, it has remained a vital protection for individual rights and liberties.

Second Amendment

The Constitution for Politicians

The Second Amendment guarantees the right to bear arms. This right is deeply rooted in American history, dating back to the country's earliest days. The Founding Fathers recognized the importance of allowing citizens to protect themselves and their families, and they enshrined this right in the Constitution.

However, the Second Amendment has also been a source of controversy and debate. Gun control advocates argue that the amendment was meant to apply only to militias, while supporters of gun rights argue that it guarantees an individual right to own firearms. The Supreme Court has weighed in on this issue, ruling in the landmark case of District of Columbia v. Heller (2008) that the Second Amendment guarantees an individual right to possess firearms.

Third Amendment

The Third Amendment prohibits the government from forcing citizens to quarter soldiers in their homes without their consent. This amendment was a response to the British practice of quartering troops in private homes during the American Revolution. While this may seem like an obscure right, it is an essential protection against government overreach.

Fourth Amendment

The Fourth Amendment protects individuals from unreasonable searches and seizures. This means that the government cannot search your home or belongings without a warrant, which must be issued by a judge and based on probable cause. This amendment is essential to protecting individual privacy and preventing government abuse of power.

Fifth Amendment

The Fifth Amendment guarantees several important rights, including the right to a grand jury, protection against double jeopardy, protection against self-incrimination, and the right to due process of law. These rights are crucial to ensuring that individuals are not subjected to unjust or unfair treatment by the government.

The Fifth Amendment also includes the "takings clause," which requires the government to provide just compensation when it takes private property for public use. This clause is essential to protecting property rights and preventing the government from seizing property without proper compensation.

Sixth Amendment

The Sixth Amendment guarantees several essential rights for individuals accused of crimes, including the right to a speedy and public trial, the right to an impartial jury, the right to be informed of the charges against them, the right to confront witnesses, and the right to an attorney. These rights are essential to ensuring that individuals are not wrongly convicted or subjected to unfair trials.

Seventh Amendment

The Seventh Amendment guarantees the right to a trial by jury in civil cases. This right is essential to ensuring that individuals have a fair and impartial resolution to civil disputes.

Eighth Amendment

The Eighth Amendment prohibits excessive bail and fines, as well as cruel and unusual punishment. This amendment is essential to protecting individual rights and preventing the government from using punishment as a means of oppression.

Ninth Amendment

The Ninth Amendment states that the enumeration of certain rights in the Constitution shall not be construed to deny or disparage other rights retained by the people. In other words, just because a particular right is not explicitly listed in the Bill of Rights does not mean that it does not exist. This amendment was included to address concerns that the federal government might claim powers not expressly granted to it by the Constitution and to reassure the people that their rights were not limited to those specifically listed.

For example, the Supreme Court has cited the Ninth Amendment in cases involving privacy rights, such as Roe v. Wade, which established a woman's right to choose to have an abortion. The Court held that the right to privacy is a fundamental right that is protected by the Constitution, even though it is not specifically mentioned in the Bill of Rights.

Tenth Amendment

The Tenth Amendment states that powers not delegated to the federal government by the Constitution, nor prohibited by it to the states, are reserved to the states or to the people. This amendment serves as a reminder that the federal government has limited powers and that the states retain a significant degree of autonomy and authority.

The Tenth Amendment has been the subject of much debate throughout American history, particularly in the context of federalism and the balance of power between the federal government and the states. Advocates of states' rights have often invoked the Tenth Amendment to resist federal encroachment on state sovereignty.

For example, in the 1950s and 1960s, Southern states used the Tenth Amendment to resist federal efforts to desegregate schools and other public institutions. They argued that the federal government had no authority to interfere with state laws and policies, and that the Tenth Amendment reserved such powers to the states.

Conclusion

The Bill of Rights is a crucial component of the United States Constitution, and it has played a vital role in protecting individual rights and liberties throughout American history. The amendments in the Bill of Rights represent a consensus among the Founding Fathers that certain individual rights were fundamental and needed to be explicitly protected.

The Constitution for Politicians

The Bill of Rights has been the subject of much debate and interpretation over the years, and the Supreme Court has played a significant role in defining and interpreting the amendments' scope and application. Despite the ongoing debates, the Bill of Rights remains a fundamental component of American democracy, and its provisions continue to guide and shape the country's legal and political landscape.

Protecting individual rights and liberties is essential to maintaining a free and democratic society. The Bill of Rights provides a crucial framework for protecting those rights, and it is up to all Americans to uphold and defend those rights for future generations.

Examples of how these rights have been upheld in American history

The Bill of Rights, the first ten amendments to the United States Constitution, is a crucial part of American history. The Bill of Rights was added to the Constitution to ensure that the government would not infringe upon individual rights and liberties. These amendments have played a significant role in shaping American society, and they have been instrumental in upholding individual freedoms throughout the country's history. In this chapter, we will explore some examples of how these rights have been upheld in American history.

First Amendment

The First Amendment protects a range of individual rights, including the freedom of speech, the press, religion, and assembly. These rights have been upheld and defended throughout American history, often in the face of great opposition.

One notable example of the First Amendment in action is the civil rights movement of the 1960s. Activists like Martin Luther King Jr. and Rosa Parks fought for the rights of African Americans to assemble, speak freely, and protest peacefully. Their efforts helped to bring about significant changes in American society, including the passage of the Civil Rights Act of 1964 and the Voting Rights Act of 1965.

Another example of the First Amendment in action is the landmark Supreme Court case New York Times Co. v. United States (1971). In this case, the government attempted to prevent the New York Times from publishing classified information related to the Vietnam War. The Supreme Court ultimately ruled that the First Amendment protected the right of the press to publish this information, citing the importance of a free press in a democratic society.

Second Amendment

The Second Amendment protects the right to bear arms. This right has been the subject of much debate throughout American history, with arguments on both sides of the issue.

One example of the Second Amendment in action is the case of District of Columbia v. Heller (2008), in which the Supreme Court ruled that the Second Amendment protects an individual's right to own a firearm for lawful purposes, such as self-defense. This ruling has been used to support arguments for and against gun control laws and regulations.

Another example of the Second Amendment in action is the role that firearms played in the settlement and expansion of the American West. Frontiersmen and settlers often relied on firearms for hunting and self-defense, and guns became a symbol of the rugged individualism and independence that defined the American West.

Third Amendment

The Third Amendment prohibits the government from forcing citizens to quarter soldiers in their homes without their consent. This amendment was added to the Constitution in response to abuses of power by the British during the American Revolution.

Although the Third Amendment has not been the subject of many court cases, it remains an important part of American history.

The amendment underscores the importance of individual property rights and the limits of government power.

Fourth Amendment

The Fourth Amendment protects individuals from unreasonable searches and seizures by the government. This amendment has been instrumental in upholding individual privacy and preventing government abuses of power.

One notable example of the Fourth Amendment in action is the case of Mapp v. Ohio (1961). In this case, the Supreme Court ruled that evidence obtained through an illegal search and seizure was inadmissible in court, strengthening the protections of the Fourth Amendment.

Another example of the Fourth Amendment in action is the ongoing debate over government surveillance and the use of technology to monitor individuals' communications and activities. The Fourth Amendment has been used to argue for greater privacy protections and limits on government surveillance.

Fifth Amendment

The Fifth Amendment protects individuals from self-incrimination and double jeopardy, and it guarantees the right to due process of law. This amendment has been crucial in upholding the rights of the accused and preventing government abuses of power.

One example of the Fifth Amendment in action is the case of Miranda v. Arizona (1966). In this case, the Supreme Court ruled that police must inform suspects of their right to remain silent and to have an attorney present during questioning, otherwise any confession obtained during the interrogation would be inadmissible in court. This decision, which became known as the Miranda warning, was a significant victory for individual rights and protections against self-incrimination.

Another example of the Fifth Amendment in action is the case of Kelo v. City of New London (2005). In this case, the Supreme Court ruled that the government could not seize private property through eminent domain for the purpose of economic development. The ruling affirmed the right of individuals to own and control their property, and it placed limits on the government's power to use eminent domain for private gain.

The Fifth Amendment has also played a crucial role in protecting the rights of individuals during criminal trials. The amendment's protection against self-incrimination ensures that individuals cannot be forced to testify against themselves, and the right to due process ensures that individuals are afforded a fair trial with legal representation.

The Sixth Amendment guarantees the right to a fair and speedy trial, as well as the right to an impartial jury and the right to legal representation. These protections are essential in ensuring that individuals are not subjected to prolonged and unfair legal proceedings.

One example of the Sixth Amendment in action is the landmark case of Gideon v. Wainwright (1963). In this case, the Supreme Court ruled that individuals who cannot afford an attorney must be provided one by the government, reaffirming the right to legal representation for all individuals, regardless of their financial status.

The Seventh Amendment guarantees the right to a trial by jury in civil cases. This right is essential in ensuring that individuals are able to receive a fair and impartial hearing of their case.

One example of the Seventh Amendment in action is the case of McDonald's Corp. v. Steel & Morris (1997). In this case, McDonald's sued two activists for distributing leaflets critical of the company, claiming that the activists had engaged in libel. The activists invoked their Seventh Amendment right to a trial by jury, and ultimately, the jury found in favor of the activists, affirming their right to free speech and protecting them from unfounded legal attacks.

The Constitution for Politicians

The Eighth Amendment protects individuals from excessive bail and fines, as well as from cruel and unusual punishment. This amendment serves as a crucial protection against government abuse of power and ensures that individuals are treated with dignity and respect.

One example of the Eighth Amendment in action is the case of Furman v. Georgia (1972). In this case, the Supreme Court ruled that the death penalty, as it was being applied at the time, constituted cruel and unusual punishment, effectively placing a moratorium on the use of the death penalty across the country. The decision sparked a national debate over the death penalty and led to reforms in the way it is applied in many states.

Overall, the Bill of Rights has played a crucial role in upholding individual rights and liberties in the United States. These protections have been put to the test time and time again throughout American history, and they have emerged as essential pillars of democracy and freedom. While challenges to these rights continue to arise, the continued commitment to their protection and preservation remains essential to the continued success of the United States as a free and democratic society.

Funny Examples of How the Bill of Rights is Applied Today

➢ Humorous stories or anecdotes about the application of the Bill of Rights in modern society
➢ Discussion of how the Bill of Rights continues to be relevant today

While the Bill of Rights is a serious document outlining important individual rights and liberties, there are also some humorous examples of how these rights have been applied in modern American society. From quirky court cases to amusing anecdotes, these examples illustrate the importance of the Bill of Rights in protecting individual freedoms and liberties.

The Constitution for Politicians

One example of the humorous application of the Bill of Rights is the case of United States v. Rosenwasser (1987). In this case, a man was charged with violating a federal law that prohibited the use of unauthorized symbols or flags on public property. The man had hung a flag with a peace symbol on it from the balcony of his apartment, and the government argued that the peace symbol was an unauthorized symbol. However, the court ultimately ruled in favor of the defendant, stating that the peace symbol was a form of symbolic speech protected by the First Amendment.

Another amusing case involving the First Amendment is the case of Korb v. Raytheon (1994). In this case, a man was fired from his job at Raytheon for making an obscene gesture at his supervisor during a meeting. The man argued that his gesture was a form of protected speech under the First Amendment. While the court ultimately ruled against the man, the case highlights the broad scope of the First Amendment's protections.

The Second Amendment, which protects the right to bear arms, has also been the subject of humorous examples. One such example is the case of District of Columbia v. Heller (2008), in which the Supreme Court ruled that individuals have a constitutional right to own firearms for self-defense. In response to the ruling, some gun enthusiasts have jokingly argued that they have the right to own tanks and other military-grade weapons under the Second Amendment.

The Third Amendment, which prohibits the quartering of soldiers in private homes without the owner's consent, is often considered one of the least relevant amendments in modern times. However, there have been some humorous instances in which this amendment has been invoked. For example, in 2013, a man in Nevada hung a sign outside his home that read "This Property is a 3rd Amendment Sanctuary." While the sign was intended as a humorous protest against government overreach, it highlights the continued relevance of the Third Amendment's protections against government intrusion.

The Fourth Amendment, which protects against unreasonable searches and seizures, has been the subject of many humorous examples involving law enforcement. One such example is the case of United States v. Jones (2012), in which the Supreme Court ruled that placing a GPS tracking device on a suspect's car without a warrant constituted an unreasonable search. In response to the ruling, some police departments have jokingly complained that they can no longer use GPS devices to track suspects.

The Fifth Amendment, which protects individuals from self-incrimination and double jeopardy, has also been the subject of humorous examples. For example, in 2015, a man in Pennsylvania was arrested for shoplifting after he confessed to the crime during a job interview at the store he had stolen from. The man later argued that his confession was protected by the Fifth Amendment's guarantee against self-incrimination.

The Sixth Amendment, which guarantees the right to a fair trial and a speedy trial, has also been the subject of humorous examples. For example, in 2015, a man in Florida who was facing drug charges argued that he was entitled to a speedy trial under the Sixth Amendment. The man had been in jail for over a year, and he argued that the delay in his trial violated his constitutional rights.

The Seventh Amendment, which guarantees the right to a trial by jury in civil cases, has also been the subject of humorous examples. For example, in 2014, a man in Utah sued a local city for $500,000 over what he claimed was an unjustified traffic stop. The city argued that the case was not significant enough to warrant a trial by jury, but the man insisted on his Seventh Amendment right. The case eventually went to trial, and the jury ruled in favor of the city, awarding the man no damages.

Another humorous example of the Seventh Amendment in action is the case of the "hot coffee lawsuit." In 1992, a woman in New Mexico purchased a cup of coffee from a McDonald's drive-thru and spilled it on her lap, causing third-degree burns. She sued the fast-food chain for $2.86 million, arguing that the coffee was too hot and that McDonald's had failed to adequately warn her of the risk. The case went to trial, and a jury awarded the woman $2.7 million in damages. While some criticized the verdict as excessive, others saw it as a vindication of the Seventh Amendment right to a trial by jury.

The Eighth Amendment, which prohibits cruel and unusual punishment, has also been the subject of humorous examples. In 2015, a man in Kentucky who had been sentenced to prison for life without the possibility of parole for a series of robberies attempted to have his sentence overturned on the grounds that it was cruel and unusual. He argued that the sentence was excessive and that he should be released on the basis of his good behavior in prison. The court rejected his argument, noting that the sentence was within the bounds of the Eighth Amendment.

Similarly, in 2019, a man in Ohio who had been sentenced to death for a murder he committed in 1994 attempted to have his sentence overturned on the grounds that it was cruel and unusual. He argued that the length of time he had spent on death row, combined with the state's recent difficulties in carrying out executions, amounted to cruel and unusual punishment. The court rejected his argument, noting that the length of time he had spent on death row was largely the result of his own appeals and that the state's difficulties in carrying out executions did not constitute cruel and unusual punishment.

Overall, while the Bill of Rights is a serious and important document that outlines fundamental individual rights and liberties, it has also been the subject of humorous examples and unusual cases. These cases serve as a reminder that the principles enshrined in the Bill of Rights are not just abstract legal concepts, but living principles that are constantly being applied and interpreted in the real world.

Discussion of how the Bill of Rights continues to be relevant today

The Bill of Rights, the first ten amendments to the United States Constitution, continues to be relevant today as it protects the individual rights and liberties of citizens and sets limits on the power of the federal government. Despite being written over 200 years ago, the principles and protections outlined in the Bill of Rights are still essential to ensuring individual freedom, autonomy, and dignity.

One of the most significant ways in which the Bill of Rights continues to be relevant is in the protection of free speech, a cornerstone of American democracy. The First Amendment guarantees the freedom of speech, religion, press, assembly, and petition, and these freedoms have been upheld in countless court cases throughout American history. The right to free speech has been essential in protecting the ability of citizens to speak out against injustice and to advocate for change. It has also played a crucial role in ensuring that the press can operate independently and report on the actions of the government without fear of retaliation.

The Second Amendment, which protects the right to bear arms, continues to be a highly debated issue in American politics. Supporters of the Second Amendment argue that it is essential for individuals to be able to protect themselves and their property, while opponents argue that it has contributed to a culture of gun violence in the United States. Regardless of one's stance on the issue, the Second Amendment remains a relevant and highly debated topic in American politics.

The Fourth Amendment, which protects against unreasonable searches and seizures, has also remained relevant in the digital age. As technology has advanced, the government has increasingly sought access to digital communications and information, leading to debates about privacy and the extent to which the government can monitor its citizens. The Fourth Amendment has been instrumental in protecting citizens' right to privacy and limiting the government's ability to conduct surveillance without a warrant.

The Sixth Amendment, which guarantees the right to a fair and speedy trial, has been essential in protecting the rights of the accused and ensuring that the justice system operates fairly. This amendment has been particularly relevant in recent years, as concerns about police brutality and racial bias in the criminal justice system have led to widespread calls for reform. The right to a fair trial and the presumption of innocence until proven guilty remain essential to ensuring justice for all citizens.

The Eighth Amendment, which prohibits cruel and unusual punishment, continues to be relevant in debates over the death penalty and the treatment of prisoners. The amendment has been instrumental in ensuring that prisoners are not subjected to inhumane conditions and that the punishment fits the crime.

Finally, the Ninth and Tenth Amendments, which reserve rights not specifically granted to the federal government for the states and the people, have remained relevant in debates over states' rights and the balance of power between the federal and state governments. These amendments have been essential in ensuring that the federal government does not overstep its bounds and that states have the power to enact laws that are in the best interests of their citizens.

In conclusion, the Bill of Rights continues to be relevant today as it protects the individual rights and liberties of citizens and sets limits on the power of the federal government. The principles and protections outlined in the Bill of Rights have been essential in ensuring individual freedom, autonomy, and dignity, and they continue to be debated and upheld in American politics and society. As the country faces new challenges and debates, the Bill of Rights will remain an essential guide to protecting the rights and freedoms of all citizens.

Conclusion

In conclusion, the Bill of Rights is a very important part of our country's history and government. It is made up of the first ten amendments to the United States Constitution, which were added to protect our individual rights and freedoms. These rights include freedom of speech, religion, and the press, as well as the right to bear arms, a fair trial, and protection from cruel and unusual punishment.

The Bill of Rights was created because the Founding Fathers wanted to make sure that the government wouldn't have too much power over its citizens. They wanted to protect us from government oppression and tyranny.

Today, the Bill of Rights is still very relevant and important. It helps us to be free and express ourselves, and it makes sure that the government doesn't take away our rights. We should be proud of the Bill of Rights and remember how important it is to protect our individual rights and freedoms.

CHAPTER 10: AMENDMENTS 11-27

The Constitution for Politicians

I. Introduction

The United States Constitution is the supreme law of the land, providing the framework for the federal government and outlining the rights and responsibilities of both the government and its citizens. While the first ten amendments, known as the Bill of Rights, receive the most attention, there are a total of 27 amendments to the Constitution. In this chapter, we'll take a closer look at Amendments 11-27, exploring their history, purpose, and impact on American society.

Overview of Amendments 11-27:

Amendments 11-27 cover a wide range of topics, from the power of the federal government to the rights of individual citizens. Here's a brief overview of each amendment:

Amendment 11: Limits the ability of citizens to sue states in federal court.
Amendment 12: Changes the process for electing the President and Vice President.
Amendment 13: Abolishes slavery and involuntary servitude, except as punishment for a crime.

The Constitution for Politicians

Amendment 14: Defines citizenship and provides equal protection under the law.

Amendment 15: Prohibits the denial of voting rights based on race or color.

Amendment 16: Gives Congress the power to levy an income tax.

Amendment 17: Allows for the direct election of Senators by the people.

Amendment 18: Prohibits the manufacture, sale, and transportation of alcohol (later repealed by Amendment 21).

Amendment 19: Grants women the right to vote.

Amendment 20: Changes the date on which the President and Congress take office.

Amendment 21: Repeals Prohibition.

Amendment 22: Limits the President to two terms in office.

Amendment 23: Gives residents of Washington D.C. the right to vote in Presidential elections.

Amendment 24: Prohibits the use of poll taxes in federal elections.

Amendment 25: Outlines the process for Presidential succession and disability.

Amendment 26: Lowers the voting age to 18.

Amendment 27: Limits Congress's ability to change its own pay.

Importance of Understanding Amendments 11-27:

While the first ten amendments of the Constitution (the Bill of Rights) are well-known, the remaining amendments are equally important for a complete understanding of the document that governs our nation. These amendments reflect the changing needs and values of American society over time, and they have had a significant impact on the rights and freedoms of individuals and the power of the federal government.

For example, the 13th, 14th, and 15th amendments, collectively known as the Reconstruction Amendments, helped to end slavery, provide equal protection under the law, and ensure voting rights for African Americans. The 19th Amendment granted women the right to vote, and the 26th Amendment lowered the voting age to 18.

Other amendments, such as the 16th Amendment (which allows for the collection of income tax) and the 18th Amendment (which prohibited the sale of alcohol), have had significant economic and social impacts on American society. And the 25th Amendment, which outlines the process for Presidential succession and disability, has been crucial in ensuring stability and continuity of government.

In short, understanding Amendments 11-27 is essential for a comprehensive understanding of the Constitution and its impact on American society. Each amendment reflects the values and priorities of its time, and each has played a significant role in shaping our nation's history and identity.

Amendment 11

Amendment 11 to the United States Constitution reads as follows:

"The Judicial power of the United States shall not be construed to extend to any suit in law or equity, commenced or prosecuted against one of the United States by Citizens of another State, or by Citizens or Subjects of any Foreign State."

At its core, the purpose of the 11th Amendment was to limit the power of the federal courts and protect state sovereignty. To understand why this amendment was necessary, we must look back at the historical context in which it was passed.

In the years following the ratification of the Constitution, there was growing tension between the federal government and the states. The federal government had been granted significant powers, but many state leaders were concerned that those powers would be used to undermine their authority. This tension came to a head in the early 1790s, when a series of lawsuits were brought against the state of Georgia in federal court.

These lawsuits stemmed from disputes over land ownership, and they were brought by citizens of South Carolina who claimed that Georgia had illegally seized their property. Georgia refused to participate in the lawsuits, arguing that the federal courts had no jurisdiction over them. The Supreme Court eventually ruled in favor of the South Carolina plaintiffs, but the case left many state leaders feeling uneasy.

In response to this case and others like it, the 11th Amendment was proposed and ratified in 1795. The amendment specifically prohibits citizens of one state (or foreign countries) from suing another state in federal court. This means that state governments cannot be sued in federal court without their consent.

The significance of the 11th Amendment cannot be overstated. It serves as a safeguard against the potential abuse of power by the federal government. By limiting the power of the federal courts, the amendment ensures that states are able to govern themselves without undue interference from the federal government.

However, the 11th Amendment has also been the subject of controversy and debate. Critics argue that it gives state governments too much power and limits the ability of individuals to hold those governments accountable. Others argue that it is an essential protection of state sovereignty and a necessary check on the power of the federal government.

In conclusion, the 11th Amendment was a response to the growing tension between the federal government and the states in the early years of the United States. Its purpose was to protect state sovereignty and limit the power of the federal courts. While it has been the subject of debate, its significance in American history cannot be denied. It remains an important protection of state power and an essential part of the Constitution.

Amendment 12

Amendment 12 to the United States Constitution was ratified in 1804, just a few years after the ratification of the original Constitution. The amendment addresses the process for electing the President and Vice President of the United States.

The Constitution for Politicians

Prior to the ratification of the 12th Amendment, the President and Vice President were elected separately, with each candidate receiving the most votes in the Electoral College assuming those respective offices. This meant that the President and Vice President could be from different political parties and could have very different views on policy and governance.

The 1796 presidential election, which was the first contested election in American history, demonstrated the flaws in this system. Federalist candidate John Adams won the presidency, while his running mate, Thomas Pinckney, received fewer votes than his Democratic-Republican opponent, Thomas Jefferson. This resulted in Adams being forced to work with a Vice President who did not share his views on governance and who was often openly critical of his policies.

The 1800 presidential election only made things worse. Democratic-Republican candidates Thomas Jefferson and Aaron Burr received the same number of electoral votes, forcing the House of Representatives to decide the winner. This led to a bitter and contentious political battle, with accusations of corruption and backroom deals flying back and forth.

Amendment 12 sought to remedy these issues by requiring electors to cast separate votes for President and Vice President, rather than lumping them together on the same ballot. This ensured that the President and Vice President would be from the same political party and would be more likely to work together effectively.

The amendment also established rules for how the House of Representatives would choose a President in the event that no candidate received a majority of electoral votes. Under the new system, the House would choose from among the top three candidates in terms of electoral votes, with each state delegation receiving one vote. This system is still in place today and has been used twice in American history - in 1824 and 1876.

The passage of the 12th Amendment was a significant moment in American history, as it helped to solidify the two-party system that still exists today. It also established clear rules for the election of the President and Vice President, which have been largely successful in preventing the kind of chaos and uncertainty that marked the early years of the American republic.

Amendment 13

The Thirteenth Amendment to the United States Constitution was ratified on December 6, 1865, and abolished slavery and involuntary servitude in the United States. Its ratification marked a significant moment in American history and was the culmination of years of struggle and activism by abolitionists and slaves alike.

Background and Historical Context:

Prior to the passage of the Thirteenth Amendment, slavery had been legal in the United States for over two centuries. Slavery was a central institution in the Southern economy, and its legacy had a profound impact on American society and culture. Slaves were considered property and were bought and sold like any other commodity. They were denied basic human rights and subjected to cruel treatment, abuse, and exploitation.

The abolitionist movement, which sought to end slavery and promote racial equality, gained momentum in the early 19th century. The movement was largely fueled by religious and moral convictions and led by figures such as William Lloyd Garrison, Frederick Douglass, and Harriet Tubman. The movement was successful in creating a groundswell of support for abolitionism and helped to spark the American Civil War.

During the Civil War, President Abraham Lincoln issued the Emancipation Proclamation, which declared all slaves in Confederate states to be free. However, the proclamation had limited effect as it did not apply to slaves in Union states or border states. The Thirteenth Amendment was necessary to abolish slavery throughout the entire United States.

Purpose and Significance:

The Thirteenth Amendment was a monumental achievement in American history, as it abolished slavery and involuntary servitude and ensured that every individual was entitled to basic human rights and freedoms. It was also significant in that it helped to redefine the relationship between the federal government and the states.

The Amendment specifically states that "Neither slavery nor involuntary servitude, except as a punishment for crime whereof the party shall have been duly convicted, shall exist within the United States, or any place subject to their jurisdiction." The amendment also gave Congress the power to enforce this provision through appropriate legislation.

The passage of the Thirteenth Amendment had immediate and far-reaching consequences. It resulted in the immediate emancipation of over 4 million slaves and changed the social and economic fabric of the Southern states. The Amendment also set the stage for further civil rights legislation in the years to come, including the Fourteenth and Fifteenth Amendments.

However, the Thirteenth Amendment did not immediately lead to equality for African Americans. Discrimination and prejudice persisted in the United States, and the legacy of slavery continued to shape American society for generations to come. The struggle for civil rights and racial equality continued well into the 20th century and beyond.

In conclusion, the Thirteenth Amendment was a pivotal moment in American history, as it abolished slavery and involuntary servitude and ensured that all individuals were entitled to basic human rights and freedoms. Its passage was the result of years of struggle and activism by abolitionists and slaves alike and helped to redefine the relationship between the federal government and the states. While the legacy of slavery continued to shape American society, the Thirteenth Amendment paved the way for further civil rights legislation and helped to promote equality and justice for all.

Amendment 14

The Constitution for Politicians

The 14th Amendment to the United States Constitution is one of the most important amendments in American history. Ratified in 1868, it was created in response to the aftermath of the Civil War and the need to address the issue of slavery and its legacy. The 14th Amendment is a cornerstone of American civil rights law and has been used in countless legal cases to protect the rights of individuals and groups.

Background and Historical Context

The 14th Amendment was ratified in the aftermath of the Civil War, which had ended just a few years earlier in 1865. During the war, the issue of slavery had become a central concern, and the Union's victory had led to the abolition of slavery in the United States. However, the end of slavery did not immediately lead to full civil rights for African Americans. In the years following the Civil War, Southern states passed a series of discriminatory laws known as Jim Crow laws, which were designed to keep African Americans from voting and participating in society.

In response to these developments, Congress passed a series of amendments to the Constitution, known as the Reconstruction Amendments. The 14th Amendment was the second of these amendments and was intended to address the issue of civil rights for African Americans.

Purpose and Significance

The 14th Amendment contains several important provisions that have been used to protect the civil rights of Americans. One of the most significant provisions is the Equal Protection Clause, which prohibits states from denying any person within its jurisdiction equal protection under the law. This clause has been used to challenge discriminatory laws and practices, including segregation in schools and public accommodations.

The Due Process Clause is another important provision of the 14th Amendment. This clause prohibits states from depriving any

person of life, liberty, or property without due process of law. This
has been interpreted to mean that the government must provide
individuals with certain procedural protections before depriving them
of their rights or property.

The 14th Amendment also contains a Citizenship Clause, which
grants citizenship to all persons born or naturalized in the United
States and subject to its jurisdiction. This clause was particularly
significant in the aftermath of the Civil War, as it ensured that African
Americans who had been born into slavery were granted full
citizenship rights.

In addition to its role in protecting civil rights, the 14th
Amendment has also been used in cases involving the relationship
between the federal government and the states. The amendment
includes a Privileges or Immunities Clause, which was intended to
protect the rights of citizens against state infringement. This clause
has been the subject of much debate and interpretation over the years,
but it has been used to challenge state laws that infringe on individual
rights.

Overall, the 14th Amendment is a critical component of
American civil rights law and has played an essential role in ensuring
that all Americans are granted equal protection under the law. Its
provisions have been used to challenge discrimination, protect
individual rights, and promote social justice. The amendment's
significance is reflected in the countless legal cases that have been
decided using its provisions and the ongoing debates about its
interpretation and application.

Amendment 15

Amendment 15 to the United States Constitution was adopted on
February 3, 1870, during the Reconstruction Era following the Civil
War. This amendment granted African American men the right to
vote and prevented states from denying or abridging the right to vote
based on "race, color, or previous condition of servitude."

Background and Historical Context

The Constitution for Politicians

Before the 15th Amendment was adopted, African Americans, particularly those in the South, were systematically denied the right to vote through various means, such as poll taxes, literacy tests, and violence. This was part of a broader effort by Southern states to maintain white supremacy and prevent African Americans from gaining political power.

During the Reconstruction Era, the federal government took steps to guarantee African Americans' civil rights, including the right to vote. The 15th Amendment was proposed by Congress in 1869 and ratified by the required number of states in 1870, becoming the third of the Reconstruction Amendments.

Purpose and Significance

The 15th Amendment was a significant milestone in the struggle for civil rights in the United States. It explicitly prohibited the states from denying the right to vote based on race, color, or previous condition of servitude, and it opened up the political process to millions of African American men who had been disenfranchised for generations.

The amendment also had a profound impact on American politics. African American men began to participate in the political process, running for office, and winning seats in state legislatures and Congress. In fact, the first African American to serve in the U.S. Senate, Hiram Revels, was elected in 1870, the same year the 15th Amendment was ratified.

However, while the 15th Amendment guaranteed the right to vote regardless of race, it did not guarantee the right to vote for all. Other measures such as poll taxes, literacy tests, and violence continued to be used to prevent African Americans from voting in many areas. It wasn't until the Civil Rights Act of 1964 and the Voting Rights Act of 1965 that these barriers were finally removed.

Despite its limitations, the 15th Amendment remains a crucial component of the Constitution's protection of civil rights and continues to be celebrated as a landmark achievement in the struggle for equality and justice for all Americans.

Amendment 16

Background and historical context:

The 16th Amendment to the United States Constitution was ratified in 1913 and gave Congress the power to impose a federal income tax. Prior to the passage of this amendment, the government relied heavily on tariffs and excise taxes to generate revenue. However, the changing economic landscape and the need for a more stable and consistent source of revenue led to the push for an income tax.

The idea of an income tax had been proposed by several politicians and economists prior to the passage of the 16th Amendment. In fact, the first federal income tax was levied during the Civil War as a temporary measure to help finance the war effort. The tax was later repealed in 1872, but the idea of an income tax persisted.

During the early 20th century, there was a growing sentiment among Americans that the wealthy should pay a larger share of taxes to help fund government programs and services. This sentiment was reflected in the passage of the 16th Amendment, which provided Congress with a new tool to raise revenue and address income inequality.

Purpose and significance:

The primary purpose of the 16th Amendment was to give Congress the power to impose a federal income tax. Prior to the amendment, the government was limited in its ability to tax individuals and relied heavily on tariffs and excise taxes to generate revenue. This meant that the government's revenue was largely dependent on international trade and the consumption of certain goods.

The income tax provided a new and more stable source of revenue for the federal government. It allowed the government to generate revenue based on the income of individuals and businesses, rather than relying solely on tariffs and excise taxes. This gave the government more flexibility in funding programs and services, and helped to reduce the country's reliance on international trade.

In addition to providing a new source of revenue, the income tax also helped to address income inequality. Prior to the passage of the 16th Amendment, the wealthy paid a relatively small share of taxes compared to the middle and lower classes. The income tax helped to shift the burden of taxes onto the wealthy, who were better able to afford it. This helped to reduce income inequality and ensure that everyone paid their fair share.

Another significant impact of the 16th Amendment was its role in shaping the modern American economy. The income tax has played a crucial role in funding government programs and services, including infrastructure projects, education, and social welfare programs. It has also helped to shape economic policy, as lawmakers have used tax incentives and deductions to encourage certain behaviors and discourage others.

Overall, the 16th Amendment has had a significant impact on American society and the economy. It provided Congress with a new tool to raise revenue, helped to reduce income inequality, and played a crucial role in shaping the modern American economy.

Amendment 17

Amendment 17 is one of the later amendments to the United States Constitution, and it deals with the election of Senators. In this chapter, we will discuss the historical context behind the amendment's creation, the purpose of the amendment, and its significance today.

Background and Historical Context

Before the passage of the 17th Amendment, Senators were not elected directly by the people. Instead, they were chosen by state legislatures. This method of selecting Senators was established in Article I, Section 3 of the Constitution, which reads:

"The Senate of the United States shall be composed of two Senators from each State, chosen by the Legislature thereof, for six Years; and each Senator shall have one Vote."

This method of selecting Senators was seen as a way to balance the power between the federal government and the states. However, over time, it became a subject of controversy. Critics argued that the system allowed state legislatures to be influenced by special interests, leading to corrupt practices and undermining the democratic process.

In addition, the system created problems for some states. In the late 19th century, the political party in control of the state legislature often controlled the Senate seats. This meant that states with closely divided legislatures might not have any representation in the Senate. It also allowed for situations in which state legislatures would deadlock over the selection of a Senator, leaving the seat vacant.

These issues led to a growing movement for direct election of Senators. The movement gained momentum during the Progressive Era, which was a time of reform in the late 19th and early 20th centuries. Progressives believed that direct election of Senators would be a way to combat political corruption and promote transparency in government.

Purpose and Significance

The 17th Amendment was proposed by Congress in 1912 and was ratified by the states in 1913. It established the direct election of Senators by the people of each state. The text of the amendment reads:

"The Senate of the United States shall be composed of two Senators from each state, elected by the people thereof, for six years; and each Senator shall have one vote. The electors in each state shall have the qualifications requisite for electors of the most numerous branch of the state legislatures."

The purpose of the amendment was to increase the democratic representation of citizens in the federal government. By allowing citizens to directly elect their Senators, the amendment aimed to eliminate the influence of special interests and prevent corrupt practices in the selection of Senators. It also aimed to ensure that all states were equally represented in the Senate, regardless of the political makeup of their legislatures.

The amendment had an immediate impact on the political landscape of the United States. Direct election of Senators gave citizens a greater voice in the federal government and made Senators more accountable to the people they represent. It also helped to reduce corruption and promote transparency in government.

Today, the 17th Amendment remains an important part of the Constitution. It has helped to ensure that the Senate is more representative of the people and has reduced the influence of special interests in the selection of Senators. However, some critics argue that the amendment has also led to an increase in partisanship in the Senate, as Senators are now more directly accountable to their political parties and to their constituents.

Conclusion

In conclusion, the 17th Amendment was a significant change to the Constitution that helped to promote democracy and transparency in the federal government. By allowing citizens to directly elect their Senators, the amendment eliminated the influence of special interests and ensured that all states were equally represented in the Senate. Today, the amendment remains an important part of the Constitution and continues to shape the political landscape of the United States.

Amendment 18

Background and Historical Context of the 18th Amendment:

The 18th Amendment, also known as the Prohibition Amendment, was passed by Congress on December 18, 1917, and ratified on January 16, 1919. It prohibited the manufacturing, sale, and transportation of alcoholic beverages in the United States. The amendment was a culmination of the temperance movement that had been growing in the United States since the mid-19th century. Supporters of the temperance movement believed that alcohol consumption was responsible for many of the country's social problems, including crime, poverty, and domestic violence.

During the late 19th and early 20th centuries, the temperance movement gained momentum as women's suffrage groups and religious organizations joined the cause. The Anti-Saloon League, founded in 1893, became one of the most influential temperance groups, advocating for prohibition at the state and federal levels. In 1917, President Woodrow Wilson declared that the United States needed to conserve food and grain for the war effort, and he urged Congress to pass a prohibition amendment to save these resources.

Purpose and Significance of the 18th Amendment:

The purpose of the 18th Amendment was to reduce the consumption of alcohol and its associated social problems. Supporters of the amendment believed that prohibiting alcohol would lead to a more productive and moral society. However, the amendment had unintended consequences. It led to the rise of organized crime and illegal speakeasies, which distributed alcohol to those who wanted it. It also led to a rise in corruption, as law enforcement officers and government officials were bribed to turn a blind eye to the illegal activities.

The 18th Amendment was repealed by the 21st Amendment on December 5, 1933. The repeal of the 18th Amendment was a recognition of the failure of Prohibition and the negative impact it had on American society. The repeal was supported by many who believed that it was a violation of personal liberty and that it had caused more harm than good.

Repeal with the 21st Amendment:

The 21st Amendment, which repealed the 18th Amendment, was ratified on December 5, 1933. The 21st Amendment gave each state the power to regulate the sale and distribution of alcoholic beverages within its borders. The amendment also legalized the production and sale of beer and wine with an alcohol content of less than 3.2%. This amendment effectively ended Prohibition and allowed the legal sale of alcohol in the United States.

The repeal of the 18th Amendment was a long and difficult process. The Great Depression had devastated the American economy, and many believed that legalizing alcohol would provide a much-needed boost. The repeal effort was also supported by the Catholic Church, which had been a strong opponent of Prohibition. The Catholic Church believed that Prohibition had led to an increase in organized crime and corruption, and that it violated individual freedom and personal liberty.

In 1932, Franklin D. Roosevelt campaigned for the presidency on a platform that included the repeal of Prohibition. He argued that Prohibition had failed to achieve its goals and that it had created more problems than it had solved. After he was elected, Roosevelt signed the Cullen-Harrison Act, which legalized the sale of beer and wine with an alcohol content of less than 3.2%. This act was the first step towards the repeal of Prohibition.

Conclusion:

The 18th Amendment was an attempt to address the perceived social problems associated with alcohol consumption. However, it had unintended consequences that led to a rise in organized crime, corruption, and violence. The 21st Amendment repealed the 18th Amendment and gave each state the power to regulate the sale and distribution of alcoholic beverages within its borders. The repeal of the 18th Amendment is an example of the Constitution's ability to adapt to changing circumstances and correct mistakes made in the past.

Furthermore, the 18th Amendment and its subsequent repeal highlight the importance of balancing individual freedoms with the need for public health and safety. While the amendment sought to protect the well-being of citizens, it ultimately infringed upon their personal liberty and autonomy. The repeal of the amendment demonstrated the recognition of this balance and the importance of protecting individual rights.

Overall, the 18th Amendment and its eventual repeal serve as a reminder of the complexity of governing and the importance of careful consideration when enacting laws and amendments. The Constitution and its amendments must serve the needs and rights of the people, and the 21st Amendment serves as an example of how correcting mistakes can ultimately strengthen the principles of democracy and protect individual liberties.

Amendment 19

Introduction:

The 19th Amendment to the United States Constitution was a landmark achievement in the fight for women's suffrage. It granted women the right to vote, a right that had been denied to them for over a century. In this chapter, we will explore the background and historical context of the 19th Amendment, as well as its purpose and significance.

Background and Historical Context:

The struggle for women's suffrage began in the mid-19th century, when women first started to organize and agitate for their rights. Women were excluded from political life, denied the right to own property, and had limited educational and employment opportunities. Despite these obstacles, women formed organizations such as the National Woman Suffrage Association and the American Woman Suffrage Association to advocate for their cause.

The suffrage movement gained momentum in the late 19th and early 20th centuries, with women staging protests and demonstrations across the country. The suffragists faced opposition from many quarters, including politicians, religious leaders, and even some women who believed that it was not proper for women to engage in politics.

The Constitution for Politicians

The suffrage movement gained a boost during World War I, when women stepped up to fill many of the jobs that had been left vacant by men who had gone off to fight. Women's contributions to the war effort helped to change public attitudes towards women's rights and gave the suffrage movement a renewed sense of urgency.

Purpose and Significance:

The purpose of the 19th Amendment was to grant women the right to vote, a right that had been denied to them for over a century. The amendment reads: "The right of citizens of the United States to vote shall not be denied or abridged by the United States or by any State on account of sex."

The passage of the 19th Amendment was a significant milestone in the struggle for women's rights. It gave women the ability to participate fully in the political process and to have their voices heard on issues that were important to them. Women could now vote for elected officials who would represent their interests, and they could run for office themselves.

The impact of the 19th Amendment was felt immediately. In the 1920 presidential election, millions of women cast their ballots for the first time. Women began to serve in political offices at all levels of government, and their participation in politics helped to bring about significant social and political changes.

The passage of the 19th Amendment also had a ripple effect on other areas of women's rights. Women began to demand greater educational and employment opportunities, and they fought for equal pay and equal rights in the workplace. The 19th Amendment paved the way for the women's rights movement of the 1960s and 1970s, which led to the passage of laws such as Title IX and the Equal Pay Act.

Conclusion:

The 19th Amendment to the United States Constitution was a landmark achievement in the fight for women's suffrage. It granted women the right to vote, a right that had been denied to them for over a century. The passage of the 19th Amendment was a significant milestone in the struggle for women's rights and had a profound impact on American society. Women gained the ability to participate fully in the political process and to have their voices heard on issues that were important to them. The 19th Amendment paved the way for the women's rights movement of the 1960s and 1970s and continues to be celebrated as a symbol of progress and equality in the United States.

Amendment 20

Background and Historical Context

The 20th Amendment to the United States Constitution, also known as the "Lame Duck Amendment," was ratified on January 23, 1933, and became effective on October 15 of the same year. The amendment was proposed in response to the problems that arose during the transition period between presidential administrations.

Before the 20th Amendment, the presidential term began on March 4, following the election in November of the previous year. This meant that there was a period of four months during which the outgoing president was still in office, but the president-elect had already been chosen. This period was known as the "lame duck" period.

During the lame duck period, the outgoing president and Congress were still in power, and they had the ability to make decisions that could affect the incoming administration. This created a potentially dangerous situation, as the outgoing officials may not have had the same priorities as the incoming officials.

Purpose and Significance

The 20th Amendment was proposed to address these concerns by shortening the lame duck period and establishing a clear timeline for the transfer of power. The amendment changed the date of the presidential inauguration from March 4 to January 20, and the start of the congressional session from March to January 3.

The amendment also established a provision for cases where the president-elect dies before taking office. In such cases, the vice president-elect becomes president on January 20.

One of the most significant effects of the 20th Amendment was the reduction of the lame duck period from four months to just over two months. This reduced the amount of time during which outgoing officials could make decisions that could affect the incoming administration.

The amendment also established a clear timeline for the transfer of power, which helped to ensure a smooth transition from one administration to the next. This was particularly important during times of crisis, such as during World War II, when a quick and efficient transfer of power was essential.

The 20th Amendment also had important implications for congressional elections. By moving the start of the congressional session to January 3, the amendment ensured that newly-elected members of Congress could take office more quickly and get to work on important issues.

In conclusion, the 20th Amendment was a significant addition to the Constitution that helped to address the problems associated with the lame duck period. By shortening the transition period and establishing a clear timeline for the transfer of power, the amendment helped to ensure a smooth and efficient transfer of power between presidential administrations. The amendment also had important implications for congressional elections and helped to ensure that newly-elected members of Congress could take office more quickly and get to work on important issues.

Amendment 21

Background and historical context:

The 21st Amendment to the United States Constitution is perhaps one of the most significant amendments in American history. It was ratified on December 5, 1933, and repealed the 18th Amendment, which had banned the manufacture, sale, and transportation of alcohol in the United States. The 18th Amendment was passed in 1919 in response to a social movement called the temperance movement, which sought to ban alcohol consumption altogether.

However, the Prohibition era that followed was rife with corruption, organized crime, and public defiance of the law. It became clear that the 18th Amendment was not effective in achieving its intended goal of reducing social ills related to alcohol consumption, and instead, it caused more problems than it solved. The repeal of the 18th Amendment and the passage of the 21st Amendment were a significant turning point in American history, as it marked the end of a failed social experiment and the restoration of individual rights.

Purpose and significance:

The 21st Amendment to the United States Constitution is significant because it repealed the 18th Amendment, which had been in effect for over a decade. The 18th Amendment had banned the manufacture, sale, and transportation of alcohol in the United States, with the intention of reducing social ills related to alcohol consumption such as crime, poverty, and family breakdown.

However, the Prohibition era that followed was marked by a rise in organized crime, corruption, and violence. Bootlegging became a profitable underground industry, and speakeasies (illegal drinking establishments) became popular. In addition, the ban on alcohol created a black market that was difficult for law enforcement to control, leading to widespread corruption and organized crime.

The repeal of the 18th Amendment through the 21st Amendment was significant because it recognized the failure of Prohibition and restored individual rights. The 21st Amendment gave each state the power to regulate the sale and distribution of alcoholic beverages within its borders, effectively ending the federal ban on alcohol. This gave individuals the freedom to consume alcohol responsibly and legally, and allowed states to regulate the sale and distribution of alcohol based on their own laws and values.

In addition, the 21st Amendment was significant because it demonstrated the power of the people to influence government policy. The temperance movement, which had advocated for the ban on alcohol, was a powerful social movement that had garnered significant public support. However, the failure of Prohibition and the subsequent repeal of the 18th Amendment was a clear demonstration that even popular social movements could be misguided, and that individual rights should always be protected.

Repeal of the 18th Amendment:

The 21st Amendment repealed the 18th Amendment and effectively ended Prohibition. It gave each state the power to regulate the sale and distribution of alcoholic beverages within its borders, which allowed for more localized control over the production and sale of alcohol. This led to a more responsible and regulated alcohol industry, which was better able to address public concerns related to alcohol consumption.

The repeal of the 18th Amendment also had a significant impact on American society. It led to a decrease in organized crime and corruption, as the black market for alcohol disappeared. It also gave individuals the freedom to consume alcohol responsibly and legally, without fear of prosecution. In addition, the repeal of the 18th Amendment helped to restore faith in the government and its ability to respond to public concerns.

Conclusion:

The 21st Amendment to the United States Constitution is a significant amendment that repealed the failed 18th Amendment and restored individual rights. The Prohibition era that followed the passage of the 18th Amendment was marked by corruption, organized crime, and violence, and it became clear that the ban on alcohol was not effective in achieving its intended goals. The 21st Amendment returned power to the states to regulate alcohol as they saw fit, and allowed individuals the freedom to make their own choices regarding the consumption of alcoholic beverages.

The repeal of the 18th Amendment was a significant victory for individual liberties and state autonomy. It also demonstrated the power of the democratic process to correct past mistakes and adjust policies in response to changing circumstances.

The 21st Amendment has had a lasting impact on American society, not only by ending the failed experiment of Prohibition, but also by cementing the idea that individual rights and state power are fundamental to the American system of government. The amendment serves as a reminder of the importance of balancing individual liberties with the need for regulation and the role of the states in governing their own affairs.

In summary, the 21st Amendment is a testament to the resilience of the American democratic process and the commitment to individual liberties and state autonomy. It corrected a mistake made by the government in the past and restored individual freedoms, while also recognizing the important role of the states in governing their own affairs. The repeal of the 18th Amendment and the passage of the 21st Amendment have had a lasting impact on American society and remain a significant part of our constitutional history.

Amendment 22

he 22nd Amendment to the United States Constitution is a relatively recent amendment, having been ratified in 1951. This amendment sets limits on the number of terms a president can serve in office. In this chapter, we will explore the background and historical context of the 22nd Amendment, as well as its purpose and significance.

Background and Historical Context

The 22nd Amendment to the Constitution was born out of a tradition that was established by the nation's first president, George

Washington. After serving two terms in office, Washington declined to run for a third term, setting a precedent that would last until the 20th century.

The idea of term limits gained more traction in the aftermath of President Franklin D. Roosevelt's four-term presidency. Roosevelt, who had been elected to office four times between 1932 and 1944, died in office in 1945, prompting Congress to consider whether it was necessary to limit the number of terms a president could serve.

In 1947, Congress passed the 22nd Amendment, which proposed limiting presidents to two terms. The amendment was ratified by the necessary number of states in 1951, making it a part of the United States Constitution.

Purpose and Significance

The primary purpose of the 22nd Amendment is to prevent a president from serving more than two terms in office. The idea behind this is to limit the power of the executive branch and prevent any one person from becoming too powerful.

The amendment is also significant because it reinforces the idea that the United States is a democracy, not a monarchy or dictatorship. By limiting the number of terms a president can serve, the United States ensures that no one person or party can gain too much power and that the will of the people is upheld.

Furthermore, the 22nd Amendment promotes fairness and equality in the political process. By setting term limits, the amendment ensures that there is turnover in the presidency, which allows for new ideas and fresh perspectives to be brought to the table. This encourages a more competitive political environment and ensures that no one person or party becomes too entrenched in power.

In addition, the 22nd Amendment has helped to solidify the role of the vice president in the presidential succession process. Prior to the amendment's passage, there was no clear protocol for what would happen if a president died or became incapacitated while in office.

The 22nd Amendment established that the vice president would take over as president in such situations, providing a clear and stable plan of succession.

Overall, the 22nd Amendment has played a crucial role in maintaining a balance of power in the United States government. By preventing any one person from serving as president for too long, the amendment ensures that the country remains a democracy in which the will of the people is always upheld.

Amendment 23

Background and historical context

The 23rd Amendment to the United States Constitution was ratified on March 29, 1961, and it grants citizens of the District of Columbia the right to vote in presidential elections. Prior to the amendment's passage, residents of D.C. were excluded from voting in presidential elections, despite being subject to federal taxes and laws. The 23rd Amendment was a significant step towards granting full voting rights to all American citizens, regardless of where they live.

The movement for voting rights for residents of D.C. gained momentum in the early 20th century, as the city's population grew and its residents began to demand greater representation in government. In 1940, Congress passed a law allowing residents of D.C. to vote in presidential elections, but the law was quickly challenged in court and ultimately struck down as unconstitutional.

The issue of voting rights for D.C. residents continued to be debated in the decades that followed, and it became a key part of the broader civil rights movement of the 1960s. The passage of the 23rd Amendment was seen as a significant victory for civil rights advocates and a step towards greater equality and representation for all American citizens.

Purpose and significance

The purpose of the 23rd Amendment was to grant voting rights to residents of the District of Columbia, who had long been excluded from the democratic process despite being American citizens. By giving D.C. residents the right to vote in presidential elections, the amendment helped to ensure that they had a voice in the selection of the nation's leader and a say in the direction of the country.

The significance of the 23rd Amendment is that it represents a crucial step towards greater equality and representation for all American citizens, regardless of where they live. The exclusion of D.C. residents from the democratic process was seen as a fundamental injustice, and the passage of the amendment helped to address this issue.

Furthermore, the passage of the 23rd Amendment helped to strengthen the broader civil rights movement of the 1960s. By demonstrating that change was possible and that progress could be made through peaceful means, the amendment served as an inspiration to those fighting for equal rights and representation across the country.

In addition to its symbolic significance, the 23rd Amendment also has practical implications for the political landscape of the United States. With the inclusion of D.C. residents in presidential elections, the city has become an increasingly important political battleground, with candidates from both major parties vying for support in the district.

Overall, the 23rd Amendment is an important and meaningful addition to the United States Constitution, and it serves as a reminder of the ongoing struggle for equal rights and representation in American society.

Amendment 24

Background and Historical Context

Amendment 24 to the United States Constitution was ratified on January 23, 1964. It is one of the three amendments to the

Constitution that were ratified during the 1960s, a period marked by significant social and political change in the country. The 24th Amendment is specifically related to the right to vote in federal elections and prohibits the use of poll taxes.

Prior to the passage of this amendment, some states had implemented poll taxes, which were a fee that voters were required to pay in order to vote in an election. Poll taxes were used primarily in the South to discourage African Americans and poor whites from voting. Since many people could not afford to pay the tax, it effectively prevented them from exercising their right to vote.

The use of poll taxes was challenged in court in the early 20th century, but it wasn't until the civil rights movement of the 1950s and 1960s that significant progress was made in ending the practice. The 24th Amendment was proposed in response to this movement, and it was ultimately ratified by Congress and the states.

Purpose and Significance

The purpose of the 24th Amendment was to eliminate poll taxes as a barrier to voting in federal elections. Specifically, the amendment states that "the right of citizens of the United States to vote in any primary or other election for President or Vice President, for electors for President or Vice President, or for Senator or Representative in Congress, shall not be denied or abridged by the United States or any State by reason of failure to pay any poll tax or other tax."

By prohibiting the use of poll taxes, the 24th Amendment helped to ensure that all citizens had equal access to the ballot box. This was particularly significant for African Americans, who had been systematically disenfranchised in the South through various means, including poll taxes.

The 24th Amendment also had broader implications for voting rights in general. By affirming the right to vote and eliminating a significant barrier to exercising that right, the amendment helped to pave the way for other efforts to expand access to the ballot box, including the Voting Rights Act of 1965.

In addition to its impact on voting rights, the 24th Amendment was significant in another way. It was the first amendment to the Constitution to address voting rights since the ratification of the 15th Amendment in 1870, which prohibited the denial of the right to vote based on race, color, or previous condition of servitude. The long gap between these two amendments highlights the challenges and slow progress in expanding voting rights in the United States.

Impact and Legacy

The passage of the 24th Amendment had a significant impact on voting rights in the United States. By eliminating poll taxes, the amendment helped to remove a major obstacle to voting for many citizens, particularly African Americans and poor whites in the South. It also helped to strengthen the principle of one person, one vote, which is a cornerstone of democracy.

The 24th Amendment paved the way for other efforts to expand voting rights, including the Voting Rights Act of 1965. This landmark legislation was signed into law by President Lyndon B. Johnson just months after the ratification of the 24th Amendment. The Voting Rights Act was a sweeping federal law that aimed to remove all barriers to voting, including literacy tests, intimidation, and other forms of discrimination.

Together, the 24th Amendment and the Voting Rights Act helped to transform American democracy by making it more inclusive and representative. They helped to ensure that all citizens had equal access to the ballot box, regardless of race, color, or wealth.

In recent years, however, there have been efforts to restrict voting rights in various parts of the country. Some states have introduced voter ID laws, reduced early voting periods, and limited the use of mail-in ballots, among other measures. These efforts have been criticized by many as attempts to suppress the votes of certain groups, such as minorities, the elderly, and low-income individuals.

The debate over voting rights continues to be a contentious issue in American politics, and the 24th Amendment remains an important tool in the fight for equal access to the ballot box. While progress has been made since its passage, there is still much work to be done to ensure that all citizens have the right to vote and have their voices heard in the democratic process.

One of the key arguments made by proponents of voting restrictions is that they are necessary to prevent voter fraud. However, studies have shown that incidents of voter fraud are extremely rare, and many of the measures introduced to combat it have been found to be unnecessary and discriminatory.

Opponents of voting restrictions argue that they are part of a broader effort to disenfranchise certain groups of voters and tilt the political playing field in favor of one party or another. They point to the fact that the groups most likely to be affected by these laws tend to vote for Democratic candidates, and argue that the real goal of the restrictions is to limit the power of those voters.

In response to these efforts, there have been calls for stronger federal protections for voting rights. Some have suggested a constitutional amendment that would enshrine the right to vote in the Constitution itself, while others have called for the passage of federal legislation to guarantee equal access to the ballot box.

Regardless of the outcome of this debate, it is clear that the 24th Amendment remains an important tool in the fight for voting rights and equal access to the democratic process. By prohibiting poll taxes and other forms of voting restrictions based on wealth, it helped to pave the way for greater equality and representation in American politics. Its legacy continues to be felt today, as Americans continue to struggle for equal access to the ballot box and the right to have their voices heard in the democratic process.

Amendment 25

Background and historical context:

The Constitution for Politicians

The 25th Amendment to the United States Constitution was ratified in 1967, in the aftermath of the assassination of President John F. Kennedy. The amendment provides a framework for the presidential line of succession and establishes procedures for the transfer of power in the event of a presidential disability or inability to discharge the duties of the office.

The need for such an amendment became clear following the assassination of President Kennedy, when Vice President Lyndon B. Johnson became president, but there was no clear mechanism for filling the vacant vice presidency. Additionally, there were concerns about the potential for confusion or disagreement regarding presidential succession in the event of a future crisis or emergency.

Purpose and significance:

The primary purpose of the 25th Amendment is to provide a clear and orderly process for transferring presidential power in the event of a disability or incapacity. The amendment lays out specific procedures for determining whether a president is unable to discharge the powers and duties of the office, and for transferring power to the vice president in such cases.

One of the most significant aspects of the 25th Amendment is its provision for the voluntary transfer of power by a president who is temporarily unable to carry out his or her duties. Under Section 3 of the amendment, a president can declare in writing to the President pro tempore of the Senate and the Speaker of the House of Representatives that he or she is unable to discharge the powers and duties of the office. In such cases, the vice president assumes the powers and duties of the office as acting president until the president is able to resume his or her duties.

Another key provision of the 25th Amendment is its provision for the involuntary transfer of power in cases where the president is unable to discharge his or her duties due to a disability or incapacity. Under Section 4 of the amendment, the vice president and a majority of the cabinet or another body as provided by law can declare in writing to the President pro tempore of the Senate and the Speaker of the House of Representatives that the president is unable to discharge the powers and duties of the office. This would result in the vice president assuming the powers and duties of the office as acting president until the president is able to resume his or her duties.

The 25th Amendment also provides a framework for filling a vacant vice presidency. In such cases, the president must nominate a new vice president, who must be confirmed by a majority vote in both the House of Representatives and the Senate.

Overall, the 25th Amendment has played a crucial role in ensuring a clear and orderly transfer of power in cases of presidential disability or incapacity. It has helped to provide greater stability and continuity in government, and has given the American people greater confidence in the ability of their government to function effectively, even in times of crisis or uncertainty.

Amendment 26

Background and Historical Context

The 26th Amendment to the United States Constitution was ratified on July 1, 1971, and lowered the voting age from 21 to 18. The amendment was passed in response to the Vietnam War, where many young Americans were drafted into military service but were not allowed to vote in elections. The amendment was a result of a growing movement by young people to have their voices heard and to be granted the same rights as other adults.

The idea of lowering the voting age had been discussed for several years before the 26th Amendment was passed. In fact, in 1970, Congress passed a law that lowered the voting age to 18 for federal elections, but this law was challenged and ultimately struck down by the Supreme Court. The Court held that Congress did not have the authority to lower the voting age, as it was a power reserved for the states.

The movement to lower the voting age gained momentum in the early 1970s, with many young people participating in protests and rallies across the country. The issue gained national attention, and lawmakers began to take notice. In March 1971, the Senate passed the amendment with overwhelming support, and it was quickly ratified by the required number of states.

Purpose and Significance

The purpose of the 26th Amendment was to give young people a voice in the political process and to recognize that they were old enough to make decisions about their own lives, including the decision to vote. The amendment was a response to the growing unrest and dissatisfaction among young people during the Vietnam War era, who felt that they were being forced to fight and die for their country but were not allowed to participate fully in the political process.

The significance of the 26th Amendment cannot be overstated. It was the fastest-ratified amendment in U.S. history, taking only a few months to become part of the Constitution. The amendment enshrined the principle that all citizens, regardless of age, have the right to vote in federal, state, and local elections.

The amendment had a profound impact on the political landscape of the United States. In the 1972 presidential election, millions of young people cast their votes for the first time, and they helped to shape the outcome of the election. This group became known as the "youth vote," and politicians began to pay attention to their concerns and issues.

The 26th Amendment also had a significant impact on the legal landscape of the United States. Prior to the amendment, states had the power to set their own voting age requirements. The amendment established a uniform voting age of 18 for all elections, both federal and state. This eliminated the confusion and inconsistency that had existed before, and ensured that young people across the country had equal access to the ballot box.

In addition to giving young people a voice in the political process, the 26th Amendment helped to increase the overall voter turnout in the United States. According to the U.S. Census Bureau, the percentage of eligible voters who participated in presidential elections increased from 52.8% in 1972 to 56.4% in 1976, following the passage of the amendment.

The 26th Amendment also helped to pave the way for other efforts to expand voting rights in the United States. In the years following its passage, there were efforts to extend voting rights to other marginalized groups, including African Americans, Native Americans, and residents of the District of Columbia.

Conclusion

The 26th Amendment to the United States Constitution is a landmark amendment that lowered the voting age from 21 to 18. The amendment was a response to the growing unrest among young people during the Vietnam War era, who felt that they were being denied the right to participate fully in the political process.

The amendment had a significant impact on the political landscape of the United States, as it gave millions of young people the right to vote for the first time. Since its passage, young people have played an increasingly important role in American politics, and their views and opinions have been taken into account by politicians and policymakers.

The 26th Amendment has also had important symbolic value, as it represents a recognition of the importance of youth engagement and empowerment in a democracy. By enfranchising young people, the amendment sends a powerful message that their voices matter and that they have a stake in the future of their country.

However, there are still challenges to youth engagement and voter turnout, particularly among marginalized communities. Efforts to restrict voting rights and disenfranchise voters continue to pose a threat to the democratic process, and it is important to continue to fight for the full inclusion of all citizens in the political process.

Overall, the 26th Amendment is an important reminder of the ongoing struggle for democracy and equality in the United States. It serves as a powerful symbol of the importance of youth engagement and the enduring legacy of the civil rights movement. As we move forward, it is important to remember the lessons of the past and to continue to work towards a more just and equitable society for all.

Amendment 27

Background and historical context

The 27th Amendment to the United States Constitution is the most recent amendment to be added to the Constitution. It was proposed in 1789 along with the original ten amendments, but was not ratified until 1992. The amendment deals with the issue of congressional salaries.

In the early years of the republic, members of Congress were not paid a salary but were instead given a per diem allowance for their time in Washington, D.C. This changed in 1816 when Congress voted to establish a fixed salary for members of Congress. Since then, the issue of congressional pay has been a controversial one, with some arguing that members of Congress should be paid more to attract and retain the best talent, and others arguing that excessive pay leads to corruption and a disconnect between elected officials and their constituents.

The 27th Amendment was proposed as part of the original package of amendments that included the Bill of Rights, but it failed to gain the necessary support for ratification at the time. The amendment reads:

"No law, varying the compensation for the services of the Senators and Representatives, shall take effect, until an election of Representatives shall have intervened."

Purpose and significance

The purpose of the 27th Amendment is to limit the ability of Congress to increase its own pay without first facing the judgment of the voters. This means that if Congress votes to increase its own pay, the increase will not take effect until after the next House of Representatives election.

The amendment was designed to address concerns about the potential for corruption and abuse of power among members of Congress. By requiring that any change in congressional pay be delayed until after the next election, the amendment provides a check on the power of Congress to enrich itself at the expense of the American people.

The significance of the 27th Amendment lies in the fact that it demonstrates the importance of citizen participation in the democratic process. The amendment serves as a reminder that the power of the government comes from the people, and that elected officials are ultimately accountable to their constituents.

The ratification of the 27th Amendment in 1992 was also significant because it demonstrated the enduring nature of the Constitution. Despite being proposed over 200 years earlier, the amendment was still relevant and necessary in the modern era.

Conclusion

In conclusion, the 27th Amendment to the United States Constitution is a relatively minor amendment, but it serves an important purpose in limiting the ability of Congress to increase its own pay without first facing the judgment of the voters. The amendment demonstrates the importance of citizen participation in the democratic process and the enduring nature of the Constitution. While it may not be as well-known as some of the other amendments, it remains an important part of the framework of American government and democracy.

Chapter Conclusion

The Constitution for Politicians

Amendments 11-27 are important additions to the United States Constitution. They were added over time to address specific issues that arose as the country grew and changed. Here's a brief summary of each amendment:

11th Amendment: This amendment limits the ability of citizens to sue states in federal court.

12th Amendment: This amendment changed the way that the President and Vice President are elected.

13th Amendment: This amendment abolished slavery and involuntary servitude.

14th Amendment: This amendment granted citizenship to all people born or naturalized in the United States and provided equal protection under the law.

15th Amendment: This amendment prohibits denying citizens the right to vote based on race, color, or previous condition of servitude.

16th Amendment: This amendment gave the federal government the power to collect income taxes.

17th Amendment: This amendment allowed for the direct election of Senators by the people.

18th Amendment: This amendment prohibited the sale, transportation, and manufacture of alcohol.

19th Amendment: This amendment granted women the right to vote.

20th Amendment: This amendment changed the start date of the President's term and set new rules for Congress.

The Constitution for Politicians

21st Amendment: This amendment repealed the 18th Amendment and allowed for the regulation of alcohol sales by the states.

22nd Amendment: This amendment limited the number of terms a President could serve.

23rd Amendment: This amendment granted citizens of Washington D.C. the right to vote in Presidential elections.

24th Amendment: This amendment prohibited poll taxes, which were fees charged to voters in some states.

25th Amendment: This amendment established rules for Presidential succession and the ability to remove a President who is unable to carry out their duties.

26th Amendment: This amendment lowered the voting age to 18.

27th Amendment: This amendment limits Congress's ability to change its own pay.

It's important to understand these amendments because they help protect our individual rights and shape the way our government functions. The Constitution is the foundation of our country's laws and system of government, and it's important for citizens to understand its contents in order to participate fully in our democracy. By learning about the amendments, we can better understand our rights and responsibilities as citizens, and work together to make our country a better place for everyone.

www.ingramcontent.com/pod-product-compliance
Lightning Source LLC
Chambersburg PA
CBHW052017030426
42335CB00026B/3176